CW01176760

DRIVER'S
HANDBOOK
for the
"CHURCHILL"
INFANTRY
TANK

by Vauxhall Motors
for the
British Army

REVISED EDITION   JUNE, 1943

©2012 Periscope Film LLC
All Rights Reserved
ISBN#978-1-937684-73-0

DISCLAIMER:
This manual is sold for historic research purposes
only, as an entertainment. It contains obsolete
information and is not intended to be used as part
of an actual operation or maintenance training
program. No book can substitute for proper training
by an authorized instructor. The licensing of
operators is overseen by organizations and authories
such as the state Department of Motor Vehicles
and other entities. Operating a commercial vehicle
without the proper license can result in
criminal prosecution.

©2012 Periscope Film LLC
All Rights Reserved
ISBN#978-1-937684-73-0

DRIVER'S HANDBOOK

for the

" CHURCHILL "

INFANTRY

TANK

Revised Edition.   *June,* 1943

T.S. 167/5

DRIVER'S HANDBOOK

for the

CHURCHILL

INFANTRY

TANK

FOREWORD

This handbook provides, in brief form and in handy pocket size, a " driver's guide " to the Churchill Infantry Tank. It is not intended to replace the Official Instruction Book (which is, of course, compiled in greater detail), but is simply a resume of all the vital information required by the driver in a more convenient format for " on the spot " reference. It describes, as simply as possible, the controls, method of driving and general handling of the vehicle (pages 3 to 26). It lists dimensions, petrol, oil and water capacities and other data required by the crew (pages 59 and 60). It includes instructions for general lubrication and straight-forward routine maintenance (pages 61 to 80). And it contains a short but important list of the points which need a little *extra* care and attention if trouble is to be avoided.

A complete list of the items of stowage for all models (Churchill I, II, III and IV), fully illustrated, appear on pages 27 to 58. The stowage illustrations also provide good general views of the various models.

The maintenance section—pages 61 to 80—is divided into periods (" Daily," " Every 250 Miles," and so on) with a special section showing the operations which need to be done more frequently in dusty conditions. Lubrication and topping-up jobs are printed in ordinary type, and inspection and adjustment items are in capital letters. Most of the routine jobs necessary are illustrated, and clear references are quoted for those which entail reference to the Instruction Book proper.

In short, the Driver's Handbook contains the basic information necessary to drive and maintain the vehicle. When fuller or more detailed information is required, reference should always be made to the Instruction Book.

CONTROLS

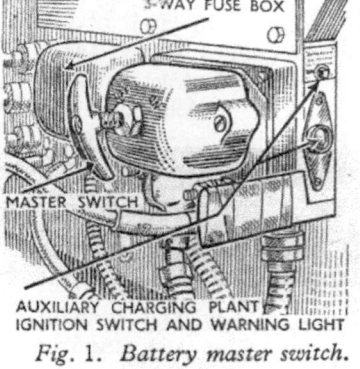

Fig. 1. *Battery master switch.*

MASTER SWITCH

Located in the battery recess. Provided to cut off all battery current from the vehicle. A green warning light glows on the instrument panel when it is on.

IGNITION SWITCH

Mounted on the instrument panel. A red warning light adjacent to it glows all the time it is switched on. The master switch (see paragraph above) must be switched on first.

STARTER BUTTON

Located in the centre of the instrument panel, and operated by pushing. See detailed instructions for starting engine on page 16.

AMMETER

Situated on the left of the instrument panel. The charging rate shown when the engine is running will vary considerably —high when the engine is started ; gradually lower as the battery is recharged. Does not register discharge.

PETROL GAUGES (2)

Near the bottom right-hand corner of the instrument panel —one for right-hand tanks ; one for left-hand tanks. The gauges are electrically operated and record the petrol level only when the push button just above them is pressed.

PETROL CONTROLS (3)

Main Tanks Control. Fitted on the left-hand " wall " of the driving compartment, near the roof. To shut off supply, move lever to extreme right. To draw on left-hand tanks move lever to " L H." To draw on right-hand tanks move lever to " R.H."

3

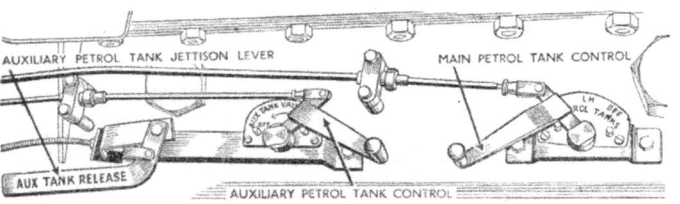

Fig. 2. Main and auxiliary petrol tank controls and jettison release lever.

Auxiliary Tank Control. Immediately adjacent to main tanks control. Keep lever in " OFF " position when drawing from main tanks. Move lever to " ON " to draw from the auxiliary tank.

Jettison Control. Situated next to the auxiliary tank control. Operates release mechanism, *and should only be moved when it is desired to jettison the auxiliary tank.*

PRIMING CONTROL

On the fighting compartment rear bulkhead—top right-hand corner. Provided so that the carburettors can be hand-primed before starting the engine. Pull out (to full extent) and push in several times before starting from cold.

" KI-GASS " PUMP CONTROL

Operating knob is mounted on the fighting compartment rear bulkhead. Three or four strokes will prime the engine

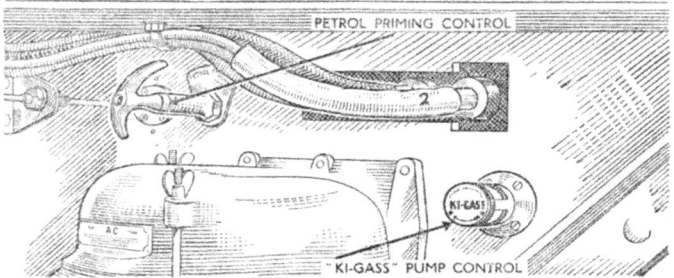

Fig. 3. Priming control and " Ki-gass " pump operating plunger.

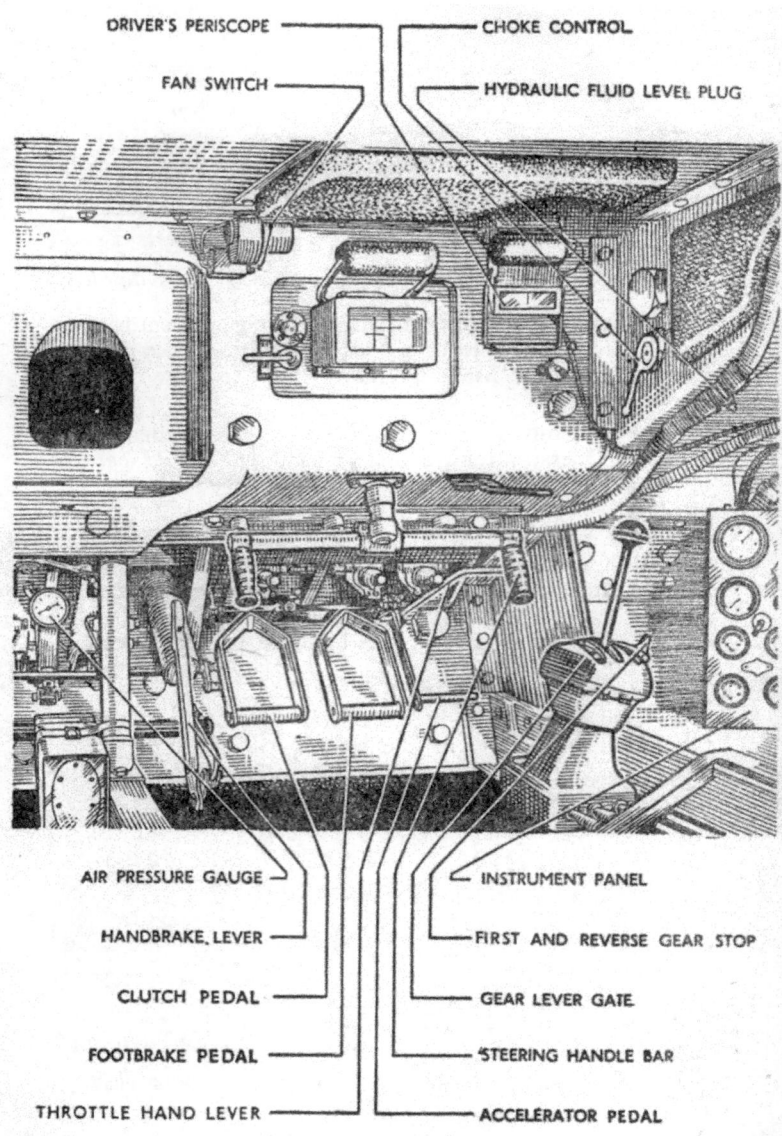

DRIVER'S PERISCOPE — — CHOKE CONTROL

FAN SWITCH — — HYDRAULIC FLUID LEVEL PLUG

AIR PRESSURE GAUGE — — INSTRUMENT PANEL

HANDBRAKE LEVER — — FIRST AND REVERSE GEAR STOP

CLUTCH PEDAL — — GEAR LEVER GATE

FOOTBRAKE PEDAL — — STEERING HANDLE BAR

THROTTLE HAND LEVER — — ACCELERATOR PEDAL

Fig. 4. *General view of the controls facing the driver. On later models a hand throttle lever is connected to the accelerator pedal.*

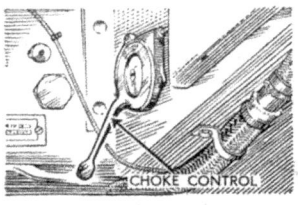

Fig. 5. Carburettor choke control.

for starting from cold. Screw the knob home firmly after use.

CHOKE CONTROL

Mounted ahead of the driver on the side wall of the vehicle. Operates the choke valves of the four carburettors. Use for starting in exceptionally cold weather only.

PETROL ECONOMY LIGHT

Located at the top-centre of the instrument panel, and labelled " PETROL." Glows when the engine is working hard and using petrol uneconomically. A good driver will aim to keep the light *out* in all normal conditions.

OIL PRESSURE GAUGE

Placed to the right of the ammeter, on the instrument panel. Records the oil pressure when the engine is running. The reading should be between 40 and 80 lbs. per square inch. Switch off and report immediately if it falls below 15 lbs. per sq. inch at normal idling speed, or 40 lbs. per sq. inch at 2,000 r.p.m., when the engine is hot.

WATER TEMPERATURE GAUGES

Two indicators for left-hand and right-hand systems respectively, located at bottom left-hand corner of instrument panel. Normal running temperature should be between 165° and 185°. Report if reading is excessive.

AIR PRESSURE GAUGE

Situated to the left of the clutch pedal. A normal operating pressure of 80 lbs. per square inch should be reached (at 1,000 r.p.m.) within 30 seconds of starting the engine.

SPEEDOMETER

Fitted in the top left-hand corner of the instrument panel. Records the ground speed of the vehicle, and incorporates a cumulative and " trip " mileage recorder. Do not exceed 10 m.p.h. in normal conditions.

TACHOMETER

This is a revolution indicator, mounted immediately below the speedometer. It registers the engine speed in multiples of 100 revolutions per minute. Reading should not exceed 2,000 in normal driving conditions. Watch this point carefully when descending hills, and do not allow the engine speed to rise above the recommended maximum.

ACCELERATOR PEDAL

The right-hand of the three foot controls. Operates the throttles of the four carburettors through a hydraulic control to the engine compartment and thence by a system of interconnected rods and levers. A right-angled lever is connected to the accelerator pedal for hand throttle operation.

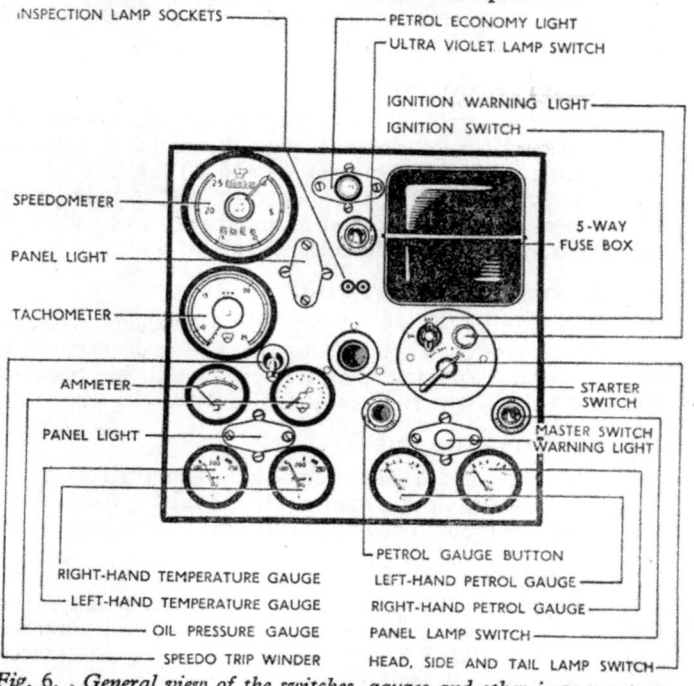

Fig. 6. General view of the switches, gauges and other instruments on the instrument panel. A convoy lamp switch is fitted to later vehicles.

7

FOOTBRAKE PEDAL

The centre foot control. Operates the main (stopping) brakes through a conventional Lockheed hydraulic system.

CLUTCH PEDAL

The left-hand foot control. Operates the clutch hydraulically and is linked up with an air pressure servo motor to provide a light pedal action.

HANDBRAKE LEVER

Situated to the left of the three foot pedals. Used as a parking brake to apply the main (stopping) brakes. If the vehicle is to be parked on a gradient exceeding 1 in 10 engage first speed gear.

STEERING HANDLEBAR

Immediately in front of the driver's seat. Operates the steering brakes through a normal hydraulic system, and is equipped with air pressure servo motors to give easy control.

Forward Steering. Pull the right-hand end to turn right. Pull the left-hand end to turn left. This is conventional practice.

Reverse Steering. *Push* the left-hand end to swing the tail of the vehicle to the left. Push the right-hand end to swing the tail to the right. This is *not* conventional, and must therefore be very carefully mastered and remembered. (See Fig. 15 on page 23).

Neutral Steering. The vehicle will pivot sharply IN NEUTRAL if the handlebar is operated. Never move the handlebar if the engine is running unless a turn is intended.

GEAR LEVER

Placed to the right of the driver. A stop in the reverse speed slot prevents accidental engagement.

LIGHTING SWITCHES

On the right-hand side of the instrument panel, below the ignition switch. The four positions are : all lamps off ; tail lamp on ; side and tail lamps on ; side, tail and head lamps on.

A separate switch (below the petrol economy light) is provided for the ultra violet head lamp, and another, on recently produced vehicles, for the convoy lamp.

The instrument panel lamps are controlled by a switch fitted below and to the right of the driving lights switch.

INTERIOR LIGHTS

Driving Compartment. Two lights are fixed to the roof, one behind the driver's seat and one behind the front gunner's seat. A switch is fitted to the base of each light.

Fighting Compartment. Three lights are fitted to the roof of the turret. Each has a switch incorporated in the base.

TELEPHONE POINTS

Driving Compartment. The driver's telephone connection is behind the driver's seat on the spot-light bin. The front gunner's connection is fixed to the roof, above and behind the front gunner's seat.

Fighting Compartment. The connection for the commander's and turret gunner's telephone is on the left-hand side of the turret, just below the cupola. The wireless operator's connection is on the right-hand side of the turret, just under the escape hatch.

VENTILATING FANS

Driving Compartment. On vehicles equipped with a Besa gun in the driving compartment, a ventilating fan is fitted immediately to the left of the driver's vision port. The switch is on the junction box near the fan.

Fighting Compartment. On vehicles fitted with a turret, a fan is mounted on the roof immediately above the Besa. The switch is on the junction box just above the turret traverse control.

DRIVER'S VISION PORT

The large door is opened by a lever just above the steering handlebar. The same lever operates the wicket door once the locking catch is released. Spring-loaded catches lock both doors in the open position, and a latch locks them when closed. All controls can be operated from inside the vehicle. To give protection to the driver when the front vision door is open, a detachable window clips into the opening.

PERISCOPES

A periscope is provided for the driver to use when the vision port is completely closed—see above. A similar periscope is provided for the front gunner.

9

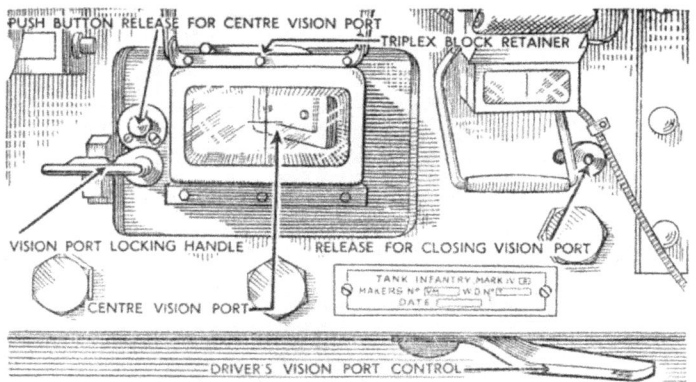

Fig. 7. *Driver's vision port and periscope*

ESCAPE HATCHES

Double-hinged doors provided in the roof above the driver and front gunner. They are fastened from the inside, but can be opened or fastened from the outside with a suitable key.

PANNIER DOORS

One in each pannier, opening into the driving compartment. These doors can be opened or fastened only from the inside. The locking device acts automatically when they are pulled to.

REVOLVER PORTS

One in each pannier door. The ports are hingeless, and are fitted with a rapid opening and closing control. Each has a locking bolt to secure it in the closed position. Similar revolver ports (two) are provided in the turret.

SMOKE MORTAR GENERATOR (on later vehicles)

The push-buttons for operating the smoke screen are on a panel mounted above the instrument panel.

MUD PLOUGHS (on later vehicles)

Fitted below the final drives, they prevent damage to the track guards by preventing mud packing in " heavy going " conditions. When not required, the ploughs can be raised from the tracks.

10

EMERGENCY CONTROLS

EXTRA STEERING CONTROL

A half handlebar connected to the main steering handlebar and located in front of the front gunner. This control enables the gunner to steer the vehicle in an emergency.

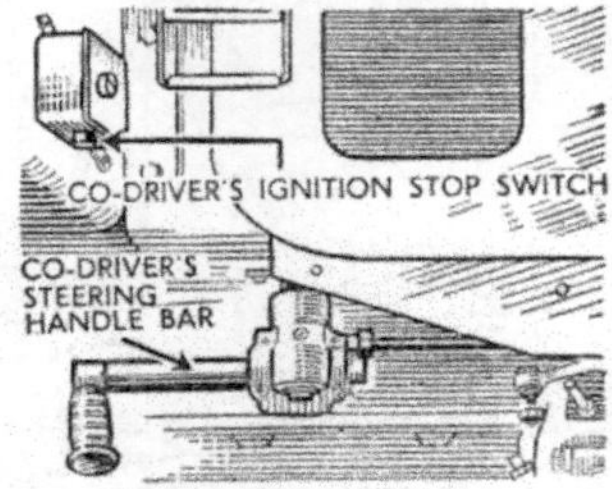

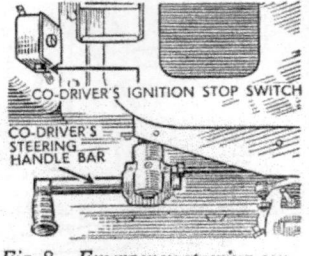

Fig. 8. Emergency steering control and ignition cut-off switch facing co-driver's seat.

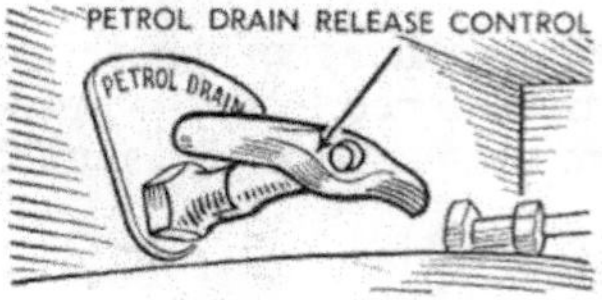

Fig. 9. Pull-out handle controlling petrol release trap.

IGNITION CUT-OFF SWITCH

On the left of the front gunner. Provided so that the gunner can switch off the engine if the necessity arises. Normally, this switch should not be touched. It is not fitted to some vehicles with a 3″ howitzer in the driving compartment.

PETROL RELEASE

A large trap in the floor of the engine compartment, operated by a pull-out handle on the rear bulkhead (near the roof) of the fighting compartment. Through this trap, escaped petrol can be quickly jettisoned.

EMERGENCY DISPOSAL HATCH

In the floor, behind the front gunner's seat. Fastened by a long-handled screw, it can be swung to one side to jettison anything not required.

FIRE EXTINGUISHER OUTFIT

2 CO_2 bottles on the rear centre of the fighting compartment, connected by pipes to nozzles in the engine and gearbox compartments. To operate, pull up the lever on top of the bottle.

Fig. 10. CO_2 operating lever and safety spring.

IT IS IMPERATIVE THAT THE ENGINE BE SWITCHED OFF BEFORE OPERATING THE FIRE EXTINGUISHERS.

The lever is retained by a safety catch which should always be removed before starting the engine.

Hand extinguishers are also provided—two on the gearbox inspection doors, one on the turret gunner's leg shield and one on the side of the miscellaneous stowage bin (front left-hand side).

FUSES

Several fuses are provided in the electrical system to protect the wiring and components.

If one or more of the electrical units fails to function, check the appropriate fuse, and if it is " blown " make sure that there is no short circuit in the system before fitting a new one.

The list on this and the facing page shows the size, location and type of each fuse, the circuit it protects, and where to look for the spares.

LOCATION AND DETAILS OF FUSES

Location	Size	Type	Location of Spares	Circuits Protected
Battery Recess (on voltage regulator).	120 amps.	Strip tin	In cover	Main regulator to dynamo.
Battery Recess (on battery panel in 3-way fuse box) (*NOTE : On earlier models the spare fuse wire in the Battery Recess is all of one gauge.* **Two** *thicknesses of this wire should be used when renewing the centre fuse*).	Top : 20 amps.	Bridge and loose wire (34 swg)	Wound round bridge	Auxiliary charging and subsidiaries (coil, warning light and petrol pump).
	Centre : 60 amps.	Do. (27 swg)	Do.	Radio, turret interior lights, turret spotlight, forward interior light and forward communications.
	Bottom : 60 amps.	Do. (27 swg)	Do.	Turret traverse excitation and turret ventilating fan.

Instrument Panel (in 5-way fuse box).	A. 20 amps.	Bridge and loose wire (34 swg)	Wound round bridge	Ultra violet lamp, forward vent fan and infantry gong.
	B. 20 amps.	Do.	Do.	Inspection lamp socket, petrol gauges, panel lights and convoy lamp.
	C. 20 amps.	Do.	Do.	Tail lamp.
	D. 20 amps.	Do.	Do.	Side lamps.
	E. 20 amps.	Do.	Do.	Plain headlamp.
Turret (in turret spotlight switch box)	6 amps.	Glass cartridge	In switch box	Turret interior lights and turret spotlight.
Driver's Compartment (in telephone and lights junction box).	6 amps.	Glass cartridge	In junction box	Forward interior lights.
Wireless Telegraph Set and Power Unit (2 fuses incorporated in radio).	Special	Glass cartridge	In wireless kit	Radio.

HOW TO DRIVE

The first part of this chapter (pages 14 to 19) explains (a) what should be done *before* starting the engine, (b) how the engine should be started, and (c) the checks and inspections that should be carried out as soon as the engine is running and before the vehicle is driven off.

In each case, the instructions are detailed in numerical sequence on one page and illustrated on the facing page.

BEFORE STARTING

The following operations should always be carried out before starting the engine. They are clearly illustrated in Fig. 11 on the facing page.

1. **Check the Engine Oil Level.** The dipstick is under the screw-type filler cap on top of the de-aerator (on the right-hand side of the engine towards the rear). On early models the dipstick is located in a tube alongside the de-aerator. Check with the vehicle on level ground.

2. **Check the Petrol Tank Levels.** Two filler caps in the gearbox compartment, one each side at the front. The tanks are full when the level is $4\frac{1}{2}$ in. below the filler caps. Do not replenish above this point.

3. **Check Water Levels.** Two filler caps in the engine compartment, one each side at the front. Securely fasten the caps after checking, as the system operates under pressure.

4. **Release CO_2 Safety Catches.** There is a safety catch on each of the CO_2 fire extinguisher bottles. The bottles are located on the fighting compartment rear bulkhead.

    Finally, make certain that the gear lever is in neutral, the steering bar straight, the handbrake on, and THAT NOBODY IS UNDER OR NEAR THE VEHICLE.

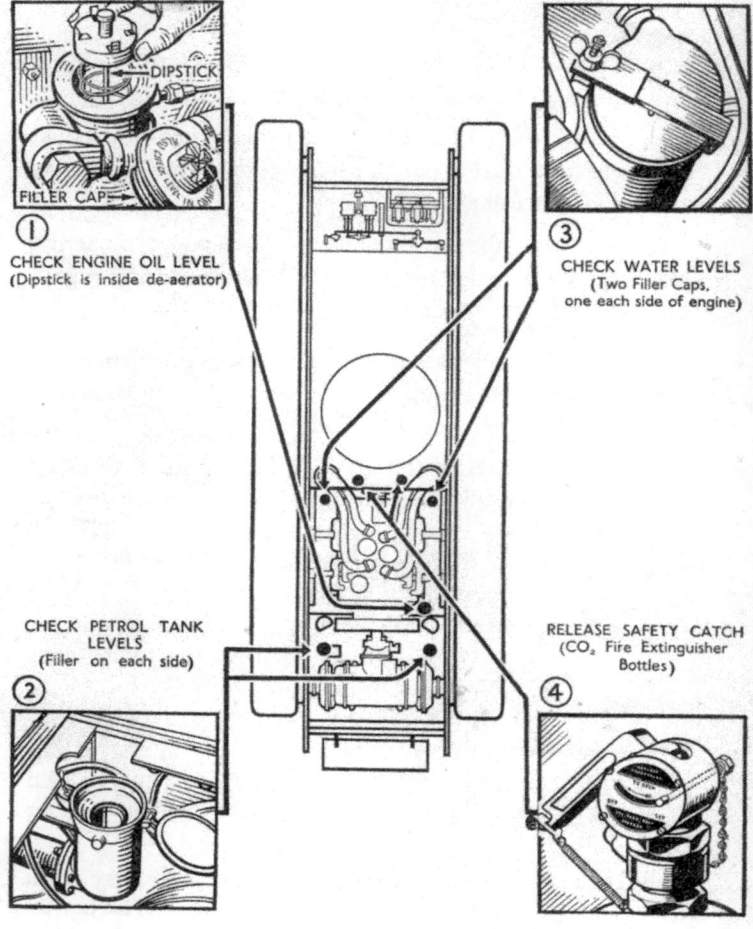

Fig. 11. *Check these items before attempting to start the engine. They are explained (numerically) on the facing page.*

STARTING THE ENGINE

To start the engine from cold, carry out the following operations in the sequence given. All the controls mentioned are illustrated in Fig. 12 on the facing page.

1. **Turn the Master Switch** (in the battery compartment) to " on." A green light should glow on the instrument panel.

2. **Turn the Auxiliary Petrol Tank Control** (on left-hand side of the driving compartment) to " on." When this tank has been jettisoned, or is empty, set the main tank control (on the left-hand side of the driving compartment) to " R.H." or " L.H." (It is advisable to operate these petrol controls once daily to ensure that they function correctly).

3. **Prime the Carburettors** by giving several strokes to the petrol priming control. (This control is located in the right-hand top corner of the fighting compartment rear bulkhead).

4. **Prime the Engine** with three or four strokes of the " Ki-gass " pump. (The operating knob — marked " KI-GASS "—is on the fighting compartment rear bulkhead. Screw it home firmly after use). Use the choke control only in exceptionally cold weather.

5. **Switch on the Ignition.** (The switch is on the instrument panel. A red light glows when it is on).

6. **Press the Starter Switch.** (The large push-button near the centre of the instrument panel). If the engine fails to start at the first attempt, wait a few seconds before pressing the switch again.

The engine should fire and run *without* the use of the petrol priming control, the " Ki-gass " pump or the choke when warm.

Running an engine for 30 minutes, on a day that the tank is not going to be used, is not recommended. The engine will only become half-warm and internal corrosion may result.

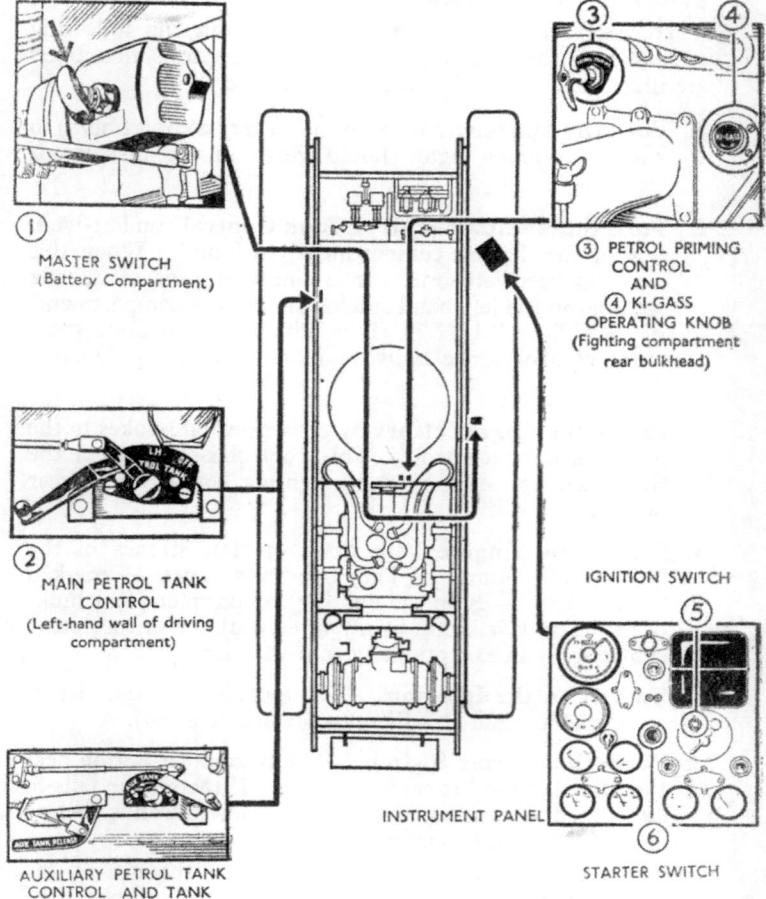

① MASTER SWITCH
(Battery Compartment)

② MAIN PETROL TANK
CONTROL
(Left-hand wall of driving
compartment)

AUXILIARY PETROL TANK
CONTROL AND TANK
RELEASE

③ PETROL PRIMING
CONTROL
AND
④ KI-GASS
OPERATING KNOB
(Fighting compartment
rear bulkhead)

IGNITION SWITCH

INSTRUMENT PANEL

STARTER SWITCH

Fig. 12. *To start the engine, operate these controls in numerical order.
They are explained in the recommended sequence on the facing page.*

BEFORE DRIVING OFF

The following checks and inspections should be carried out as soon as the engine is running. They are illustrated in Fig. 13 on the facing page.

1. **Check the Oil Pressure.** The gauge is on the instrument panel. It should register between 40 and 80 lbs. per square inch. Stop the engine and report if it registers less than 15 lbs. at normal idling speed (or 40 lbs. at 2,000 r.p.m.) when the engine is hot.

    After running the engine for 10 minutes at approx. 1,000 r.p.m., switch off, wait for two minutes and re-check the oil level. Thoroughly clean the dipstick, and add oil to bring the level exactly to the " full " mark. This additional check is necessary, as inaccuracies in reading can give a totally false figure of oil consumption.

2. **Check the Charging Rate.** The ammeter is on the instrument panel. It will probably show about 60 amps.

3. **Check the Air Pressure System.** The gauge is to the left of the clutch pedal. A normal pressure of 80 lbs. per square inch should be reached (at 1,000 r.p.m.) within 30 seconds of starting up.

4. **Check the Petrol Gauges.** The gauges register only when the button adjacent to them (on the instrument panel) is pressed.

5. **Inspect for Leaks.** With the engine running, open the engine cover doors and inspect for signs of oil or water leakage.

    If a leak is discovered stop the engine immediately and do not restart until the leak is rectified.

6. **Close and lock the Engine Cover Doors, and the Ventilation Hatch in the Engine Front Bulkhead (6-pdr. Models).** This must always be done before moving off.

    The engine front bulkhead hatch must, however, be open when the gun is being fired.

IMPORTANT.—Do not move the steering handlebar when the vehicle is not being steered. The tank will turn IN NEUTRAL if the bar is operated when the engine is running—see explanation of steering on page 22

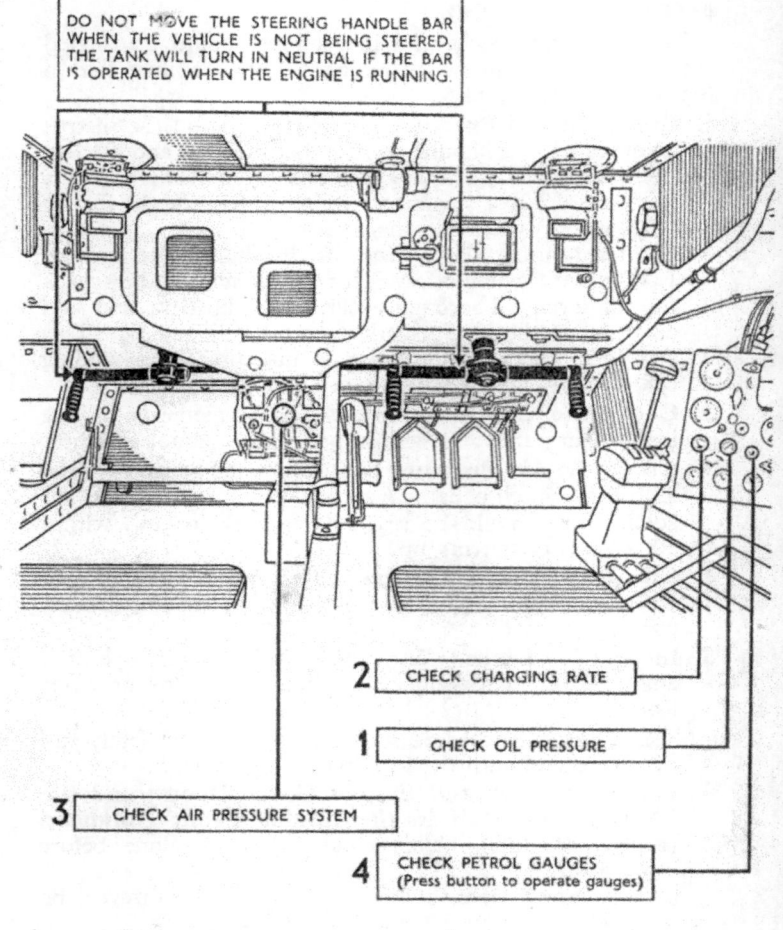

DO NOT MOVE THE STEERING HANDLE BAR WHEN THE VEHICLE IS NOT BEING STEERED. THE TANK WILL TURN IN NEUTRAL IF THE BAR IS OPERATED WHEN THE ENGINE IS RUNNING.

2 CHECK CHARGING RATE

1 CHECK OIL PRESSURE

3 CHECK AIR PRESSURE SYSTEM

4 CHECK PETROL GAUGES
(Press button to operate gauges)

Fig. 13. Check these items when the engine starts, before driving away. Normal readings and other details are explained on the facing page.

19

MOVING OFF

See that the engine idles at 600/700 r.p.m. Start in second gear (use first gear only for obstacle crossing, freak hills and towing, or when an extremely slow speed or small turning circle is required)—or if the vehicle is on a slight down grade in third.

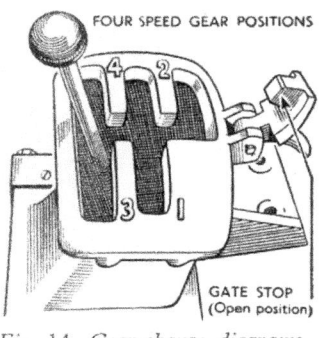

FOUR SPEED GEAR POSITIONS

GATE STOP
(Open position)

Fig. 14. *Gear-change diagrams.*

The gear change is of the normal " crash " type and is provided with a clutch stop ; the position for the 4-speed box is shown in Fig. 14. (On some early pre-rework vehicles a 5-speed gearbox was fitted).

To engage gear when stationary, depress the clutch pedal on to the clutch stop firmly but not too hard and listen for the compressor to " die down." Just before the compressor stops (which means that the clutch is also just stopping) push the gear lever firmly into the gear required. Pressing the clutch pedal on to the clutch stop very hard stops the clutch immediately and more than likely the gear will not engage. If this should happen, return the gear lever to neutral and start again, *allowing the clutch to stop gradually.*

Make sure the handbrake is fully off, engage the clutch slowly and smoothly and move off. On level ground the clutch can be engaged at the engine idling speed.

CHANGING GEAR

First to Second. This is a difficult change to do on the move, with no advantage gained. Always stop the vehicle, therefore, and change up when stationary.

Second to Third. Use the double declutch, without throttle or clutch stop, when the vehicle can roll forward at 4 to 5 m.p.h. while the change is being made. Choose a slight, but not steep, down-hill slope if possible. Don't steer while making the change or immediately after it. Rev. up in second gear to 2,200/2,300 r.p.m., take gear into neutral and pull the gear lever gently into third position when the engine revolutions have dropped to 1,500. If the tank stops moving before revs. have dropped sufficiently, start again in second gear. Should the down-hill slope be greater than estimated and the speed increase above 5 m.p.h., engage third gear at 1,700/1,800 r.p.m. for 6 m.p.h., 1,900/2,000 r.p.m. for 7 m.p.h. and so on.

To change to third on the level or uphill, with a rolling speed of less than 5 m.p.h., slow down in second until the tachometer is at 1,500/1,600 r.p.m. Make a fast racing change, using three fingers only, with full use of clutch stop but NO FORCE. Flick the gear lever across from second to third quickly but lightly. Open the throttle immediately third gear is engaged. Never use both hands to make engagement and use the slow double declutch change whenever possible to save gearbox strain. When the engine is temporarily restricted to 2,000 r.p.m., use the slow change only on down-hill slopes and the racing change more often. The engine must not be allowed to rev. up over 2,000 in second gear whilst restricted.

This change is, of course, more difficult when the box is cold and the oil thick, especially in winter. If necessary, run the vehicle for 15 minutes in second gear to warm up.

Third to Fourth. The double declutch method can nearly always be used owing to the higher maximum speed in third gear. Disengage at approx. 2,200 r.p.m. and engage fourth when the revs. have dropped well below 1,500 if the tank is still travelling at 9/10 m.p.h. If the vehicle is accelerating the gear must be engaged at higher revs.

Use the racing change if the ground is slightly uphill. Throttle back in third gear to about 1,600 r.p.m. and push the gear lever straight through into fourth with full depression on the clutch stop.

Fourth to Third. Use the double declutch, with throttle, for all changing down, as on wheeled vehicles. Little throttle is required for this change. Don't stay in top gear if the going is heavy, change to one of the intermediate gears to to ensure ample power for turning.

Third to Second. Change down when the speed is approx. 7 m.p.h. Considerable throttle is required as the engine revs. must be put up to 2,200/2,300 r.p.m. and second gear engaged at just over 5 m.p.h. If the speed is 5 m.p.h. or under, be very quick, with double declutch and less throttle.

Second to First. Normally, stop the tank to engage first gear. If in second gear and pulling up a steep bank, go on until the tank is nearly stationary, dip the clutch quickly, pull straight into first gear and re-engage the clutch quickly. Getting out of second gear after stopping the vehicle on a steep hill is not easy.

Both bottom gear and reverse gear, being very low, tend to become difficult to disengage. Put pressure on the gear lever before dipping the clutch quickly to get into neutral from these low gears, but avoid going on to the clutch stop.

General. Learn the corresponding engine revolutions for each mile per hour in the different gears. Accurate gear changing is quite simple providing the tachometer and speedometer are watched.

Do not change up on slopes steep enough to cause the tank to accelerate and never change down on a down-hill gradient. If a lower gear has not already been engaged for safety reasons on a steep hill and the gradient becomes steeper, turn slowly to the left and stop, get into second gear and re-start.

Owing to the great weight of the vehicle and the engine developing 350 h.p., mistakes in gear changing must lead to serious damage. The gearbox selector forks bend due to the pressure caused by the sliding dogs either grating against the third speed dogs or by the force exerted by the combined leverage and weight of the operating rods when moved by the change speed lever. Jumping out of third gear results from the bending of the third and fourth gear forks. The gearboxes are being progressively improved, but to keep trouble to a minimum, the use of excessive force must be avoided.

STEERING

Move the handlebar firmly and steadily, but without " snatch." Remember that additional effort is needed when operating without compressed air assistance. Always return the bar to the straight ahead position after steering.

Steering in Forward Gears. For forward steering use the steering handlebar in the same way as the handlebar of a bicycle. To turn right pull the right-hand end. To

22

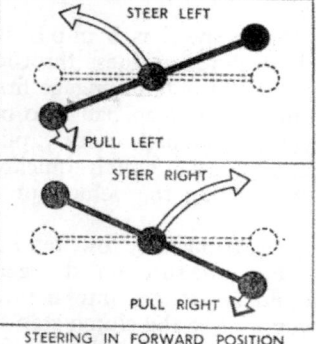

STEERING IN FORWARD POSITION

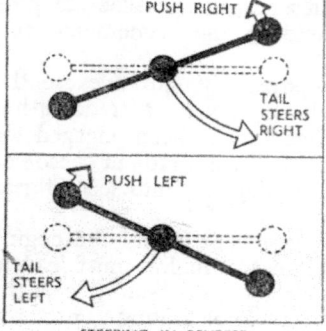

STEERING IN REVERSE

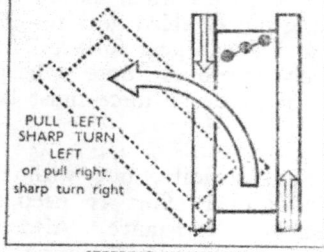

STEERING IN NEUTRAL

Fig. 15. Pictorial guide to forward, reverse and neutral steering.

turn left, pull the left-hand end.

The turning circle varies with the gear engaged. The smallest turning circle is obtained in first gear and the largest in top gear. (See Turning Radii on page 59.)

Steering in Reverse. To steer in reverse, *reverse the instructions given for forward steering. Push* the right-hand end of the bar to swing the tail to the right. *Push* the left-hand end to swing the tail to the left.

Steering in Neutral. If the steering handlebar is swung while the vehicle is in neutral (engine running) the tracks will rotate in opposite directions and the vehicle will make a sharp pivot turn in little more than its own length.

This is an extremely useful feature but it must not be misused. Never attempt a neutral turn on heavy ground, or where damage to turf is undesirable. And never move the steering handlebar when the engine is running unless a turn is intended. An unintentional pivot turn may have disastrous results.

To carry out a neutral turn, release the handbrake, accelerate *slightly*, and move the steering bar slowly and firmly

23

in the required direction (see Fig. 15, page 23). Do not speed up the engine unduly as the vehicle swings rapidly, especially on a hard surface.

General. Always endeavour to steer when the engine revolutions are high. More power is required for a turn, and if the engine speed is allowed to drop a gear change may be necessary.

Try to complete a turn with one or two movements of the steering bar. Judge which gear to be in to make a turn into any particular opening. The tank turns about its central line and does not follow the front of the track. Every time the bar is operated, power is used in operating (and wearing the linings of) the steering brake. A steady and continuous turn also avoids halting a convoy.

On uneven ground, steer when on a hump rather than when in a hollow. Avoid steering while negotiating an obstacle such as a shell-hole or a river bed.

In general, choose hard rather than soft patches for changes in direction.

OBSTACLE CROSSING

To bring the Churchill over a big obstacle without bumping, make sure that the engine idles at 600/700 r.p.m. Proceed slowly and steadily in bottom gear when crossing a shell-hole. Make sure that the gear is fully engaged. Cross the hole squarely. If it is taken at an acute angle the side thrust may push off one of the tracks.

Approach vertical walls, sleepers and similar obstacles squarely and slowly. In coming over the edge of a drop, allow the tank to creep forward with no throttle, and the vehicle will then ride over the point of balance smoothly and without jar. Do not use the brake unless there is any tendency for the tank to overrun the engine. See that the engine is never driven above the governed speed, otherwise it (and the clutch) will be damaged.

Under all conditions, the engine is sufficiently powerful to slip the tracks and will never stall due to an excessive slope or bank. Continue driving if both tracks start to slip. As the tank digs in, it may get sufficient grip to pull itself out. Failing this, take the machine back and make the run again. If after two or three attempts the tracks continue to slip, make the approach at an angle across the original marks.

BRAKES

Use the brakes intelligently. They are powerful and highly effective, but this fact should not be abused. Don't use them unnecessarily or unnecessarily harshly. Engage a low gear when descending hills to relieve the strain on the brakes. Never allow the vehicle to gain so much momentum on a slope that maximum braking effort is required to control it. Such misuse causes excessive wear, and, in extreme cases, may burn the linings and so render them ineffective.

(*NOTE.*—Take particular care, when using the engine compression as a brake, that the reading on the tachometer does not exceed 2,000 r.p.m.)

DURING HALTS

When the vehicle is halted for short periods, switch off the engine, set the petrol controls to " OFF," turn off the master switch and replace the safety catch on each of the CO_2 fire extinguisher bottles.

HARBOURING AND THE USE OF SIGNALS

If an observer is guiding the tank, which is travelling forward, he raises a closed fist to indicate a turn, using left or right according to the direction required. The driver turns the nose of the vehicle towards the closed hand.

If the tank is in reverse, the observer uses the same signals, but these refer to the tail of the machine and not the front.

For the signal stop, the palm of the hand is held up ; for acceleration, the hand is rotated.

When harbouring, remember that the vehicle takes up a lot of space and damage can be done without the driver's knowledge when the tail is swung round. When entering a narrow gateway, always make certain that the whole of the vehicle is through before turning.

AFTER THE RUN

Attend to the following points when the vehicle is parked at the end of the day's run :

Switch off the engine.

Set the petrol controls to " off."

Turn off the master switch.

25

Refill the petrol tanks.

Check water and oil levels.

Replace safety catch on each of the CO_2 fire extinguisher bottles.

Engage first gear and apply the handbrake.

Check the free travel of the clutch pedal. If it is down to an inch or less the clutch needs adjustment.

Examine the petrol, oil and water connections.

Test by hand the temperature of brake drums, final drive, suspension and bogies.

Inspect tracks and suspension for slackness and damage.

Make sure that final drive spigot bolts and coupling bolts are tight.

STOWAGE—2-PDR.
(Churchill I and II)

Illustrated on Plates A to H—pages 33 to 40.

The following is a complete list of the stowage items carried by the Churchill I and IIR. The numbers in column 1 are the numbers by which the items are identified on the accompanying illustrations. Columns 2 and 3 list, respectively, the articles carried and the number of each supplied. Column 4 contains the reference letters of the illustrations on which the various items can be found. Drawings prepared for an earlier edition have been revised for this issue, necessitating the omission of numbers 47, 48 and 54 in column 1.

VEHICLE EQUIPMENT

Item No.	Description	Number Carried	Plate Ref.
1	Fire extinguisher, CO_2—7 lb. bottle	1	D.
2	Fire extinguisher, Pyrene tetrachloride type—1 quart	2	B. G.
2a	Fire extinguisher—methyl bromide	2	H.
3	Water tanks—drinking	2	B. D.
4	Camouflage net bin :—		H.
	Camouflage net, 35 ft. by 15 ft. ...	1	
	3-piece waterproof cover for vehicle	1	
	Tent poles, 18 ins.	2	
	Tent pegs	4	
	Hemp rope, 20 ft.	1	
	Strips and disc, ground/air communication, per 10 vehicles ...	1 set	
	Matchet (15 in.) in case	1	
5	Flag bag, with 3 signalling flags (1 set)	1	H.
6	Turret headsets (microphone and receiver headgear No. 1, in bag ; includes one carried as spare in signal satchel with sling)	4	F.
7	Hull headsets (microphone and receiver headgear No. 2, in bag ; includes one carried as spare in signal satchel with sling)	3	A. B.
8	Inspection lamp	1	A.

STOWAGE—2-PDR.—continued

Item No.	Description	Number Carried	Plate Ref.
9	First aid outfit for tanks and armoured cars (packed)	1 box	B.
10	Portable cooker, No. 2 complete ...	1	C.
11	Miscellaneous bin :—		B.
	Spares and tools—Besa	1 pack	
	Suit—anti-gas (hood, trousers, coat, pair boots and 3 pairs gloves) in bag	1	
	Muzzle cover—Besa	1	
	Muzzle cover—2-pdr.	1	
	*Muzzle cover—3 in. Howitzer ...	1	
	Breech cover—2-pdr.	1	
	*Breech cover—3 in. Howitzer ...	1	
	Water bottles	5	
	Tins—biscuit, 10 oz. ration ...	15	
	Rations, No. 3. 5 men—1 day (packed)	3 boxes	
	Anti-gas ointment, tins of 8 tubes (see also No. 14, Fig. F.) ...	2	
	Haversacks, W.D. 37 Patt. ...	2	
	Gloves—wiring	2 pairs	
	Wallet for Bren gun spares ...	1	
	Pouch—Thompson sub M.G. accessories	1	
	Cotton waste	1 bdle.	
	Cleaning brush, 11 in.	1	
	Brush, bass hand, Mk. I ...	1	
	*Not required with front Besa gun.		
12	Haversacks, W.D. 37 Patt.	3	A. C.
13	Bleach powder, 2 lbs.	1 tin	G.
14	Anti-gas ointment, tin of 8 tubes (see also No. 11, Fig. B.)	1	F.
15	Anti-dim compound and flannelette	1 jar	F.
16	Shovel, G.S.	2	H.
17	Pickaxe with helve	1	H.
18	Crowbar, 5 ft.	1	H.
19	Sledge hammer (10 lbs.) with handle	1	H.
20	Water cans	4	H.

STOWAGE—2-PDR.—continued

Item No.	Description	Number Carried	Plate Ref.
21	Matchet (15 in.) in case	1	B.
22	Canvas bucket, Mk. V	1	A.
23	Map case, G.S. No. 1, Mk. I ...	1	E.
24	Wire cutters, folding, Mk. I (in frog)	1	A.
25	Hellesen hand lamp	1	E.
26	Wallet for commander	1	F.
27	Anti-gas cape and gloves	5	A. C.
28	Greatcoats	5	H.
29	Instruction book and tool lists ...	1	A.
30	Log book (Army Book AB.413) ...	1	A.
31	Hawser for towing—15 ft.	2	H.
32	Packing blocks for jack (wood) ...	2	H.
33	Auxiliary battery charging set ...	1	B.

EQUIPMENT SPARES

Item No.	Description	Number Carried	Plate Ref.
34	Prisms, object, Vickers' tank periscope	6	B. E. F.
35	Cleaning brush, prism	3	B. E. F.
36	Vision door triplex unit	2	A.
37	Spare valve bin :—		F.
	Wireless valves, 9—see Parts Tables for details	15	
38	W.T. spare parts case, No. 5 c. ...	1	F.
	Bulbs, F., 12 v., 2.4 w.	4	
	W.T. key and plug, No. 9 ...	1	
	Rotary transformer brushes (H.T.) No. 4	4	
	Rotary transformer brushes (L.T.) No. 18	2	
	Fuses (radio) 250 m/a	12	
	Holders, No. 1 caps	2	
	Adjuster screws	6	
39	Main wireless aerial	1	B.
40	Troop set wireless aerial	2	F.

VEHICLE TOOLS

Item No.	Description	Number Carried	Plate Ref.
41	Vehicle tools (see Schedule of Tools for details)	1 set	A.

STOWAGE—2-PDR.—continued

Item No.	Description	Number Carried	Plate Ref.
42	Hose—bleeding Lockheed system ...	1	A.
43	Container—bleeding Lockheed fluid	1	A.
44	Lifting jack—hydraulic—10 ton ...	1	D.
45	Jack handle	1	H.
46	Tecalemit compressor, Junior No. 2, with ball swivel nozzle, type B.S.42	1	B.
49	Spare bulb container	1	A.
	Spare side lamp bulb	4	
	Spare head lamp bulb	1	
	Spare U.V. lamp bulb	1	
50	Idler adjusting packing	70	B.
	(Less those in use)		
51	Bag, spare track pins, No. 1, containing 4 spare pins	1	B.
52	Track link (with 1 in. dia. pin) ...	2	H.
	Track link pin (includes 4 in bag, see above)	6	
	Track link pin retainer. With vehicle tools (see No. 41, Fig. A.)	6	
	Track link pin retainer lock. With vehicle tools (see No. 41, Fig. A.)	12	
	or		
	Track link (with 1¼ in. dia. pin) ...	2	H.
	Track link pin (Service) (includes 4 in bag, see above)	6	

ARMAMENT

53	M.G. Bren—.303 Mk. I	1	G.
55	Thompson sub-machine gun ...	2	B. G.
56	Signal pistol No. 1 Mk. III or Mk. IV	1	E.

ARMAMENT TOOLS

57	Piasaba bin :—		G.
	*Piasaba cleaner No. 20 with rope lanyard and lead ball (3 in. Howitzer)	1	

STOWAGE—2-PDR.—continued

Item No.	Description	Number Carried	Plate Ref.
	Bristle cleaner No. 1, Mk. I, with rope lanyard and lead ball (2-pdr.)	1	
	Cleaning rod—Bren cylinder ...	2	
	Brush, cylinder rod—Besa ...	2	
	*Sponge cap No. 6—3 in. Howitzer (container for Piasaba cleaner)	1	
	Sponge cap No. 4—2-pdr. (container for bristle cleaner) ...	1	
	Protector, object glass, in case. Spares for telescope	6	
	Grease, M.G. Mk. I	2 cans	
	Wire cutters—in frog	1	
	*Not required with front Besa gun.		
58	2-pdr. and *3 in. Howitzer tools and spares (see Parts Tables for details of Tools)	1 box	G.
	*Not required with front Besa gun.		
59	Oil can—recoil replenishment, 2-pdr.	1	E.
60	Besa spares bin :—		B. F.
	Clearing plugs—Besa med. M.G., Mk. I	4	
	Oil can—M.G., Mk. II	1	
61	Cleaning rod, .303 M.G., Mk. IIb	1	G.
62	Cleaning brush, 2 in. bomb thrower	1	E.
	ARMAMENT SPARES		
63	Striker case complete—spare ...	2	A. E.
64	Sighting telescope No. 30, in case No. 6 (optional)	1	G.
	Sighting telescope No. 33, in case No. 10 (optional)	1	G.
	AMMUNITION		
65	Cartridge, Q.F., 3 in. Howitzer wh/shell H.E. Mk. II, fuse 119, clip 9 (*Not required with front Besa gun*)	58	A.

STOWAGE—2-PDR.—continued

Item No.	Description	Number Carried	Plate Ref.
66	Q.F., 2-pdr.	150	C. D. G.
67	S.A.H. 29, Mk. I/L expendable (optional)	21 boxes	C. D.
	Belt, Besa med. M.G., Mk. I or II ...	21 boxes	E. G.
68	Bren .303 M.G. No. 2, Mk. I ...	6 drums	D. F.
69	Thompson sub-machine gun (one box in position on forward gun). 20 rounds per box	42 boxes	B. F.
70	Bomb, M.L. smoke, 2 in. mortar Mk. I	25	E.
71	Cartridge for signal pistol (8 also carried in transport)	12	F.
72	Hand grenade—Mills	6	F.

AMMUNITION REQUIRED WITH FRONT BESA GUN

73	S.A.H. 29, Mk. I/L expendable (optional)	22 boxes	B.
	Belt, Besa med. M.G., Mk. I or II (optional)	22 boxes	B.

The following items are stowed loose at crew's discretion :—

Cover—bomb thrower	1
Cover—Thompson sub M.G. ...	2
Cover—Bren muzzle	1
Funnel, collapsible—fuel	1
Filter, collapsible fuel funnel ...	1
Box—spare maps	1
Ground sheets, Mk. VIII	5
Blankets	5
Cushion seat—spare	1
Case—binoculars	1
Stretcher, ambulance, Mk. II ; and slings	2

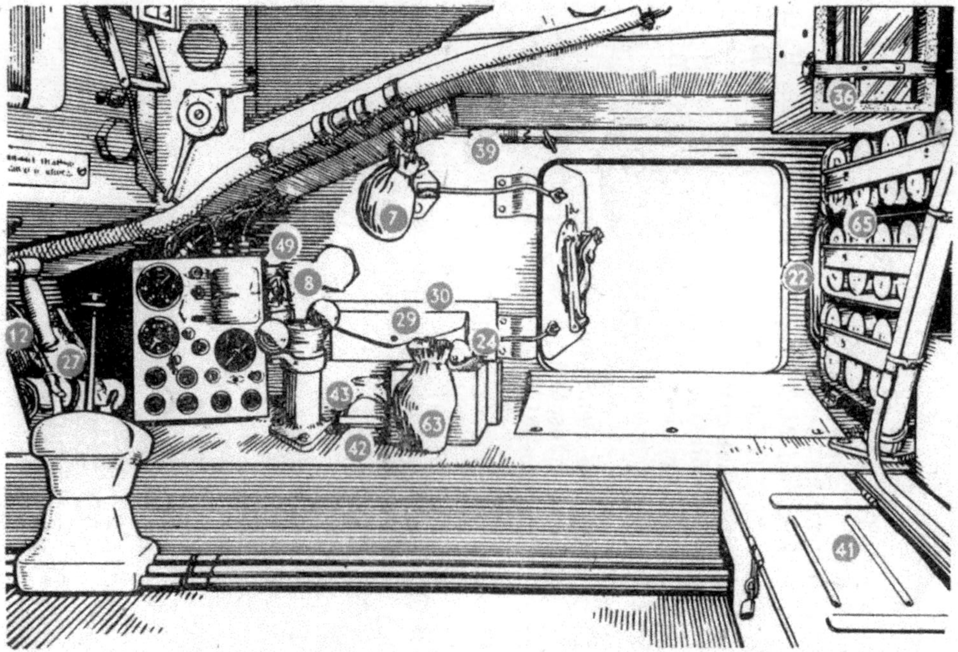

Fig. A. Churchill I and II. Driver's compartment—right-hand side. Churchill 2-pdr.

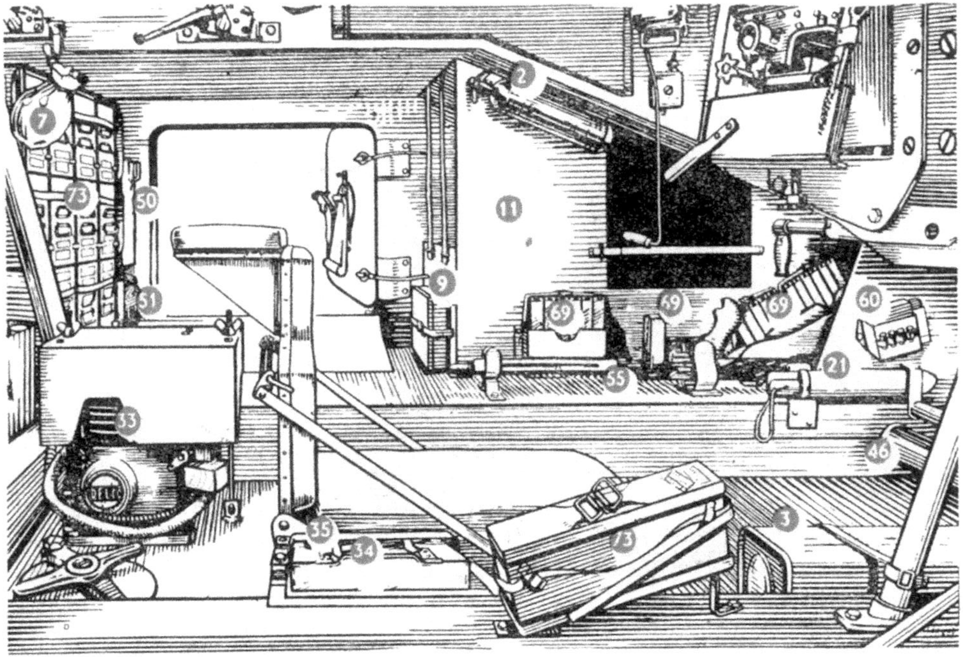

Fig. B. Churchill I and II. Driver's compartment—left-hand side. Churchill 2-pdr.

Fig. C. Churchill I and II. Fighting compartment—right-hand side. Churchill 2-pdr.

Fig. D. Churchill I and II. Fighting compartment—left-hand side. Churchill 2-pdr.

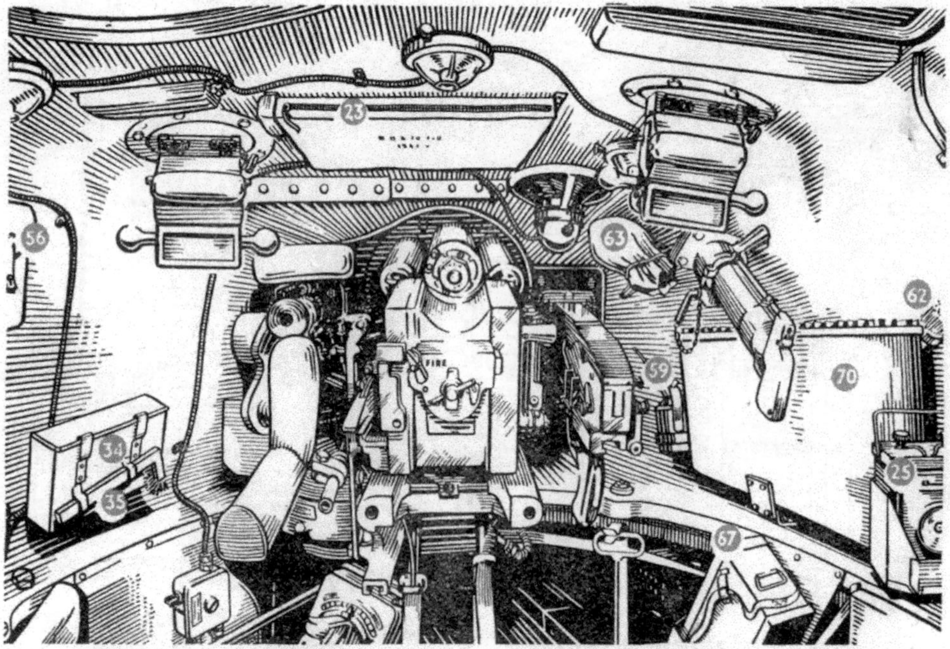

Fig. E. *Churchill I and II. Turret interior—front half. Churchill 2-pdr.*

Fig. F. *Churchill I and II. Turret interior—rear half.* *Churchill 2-pdr.*

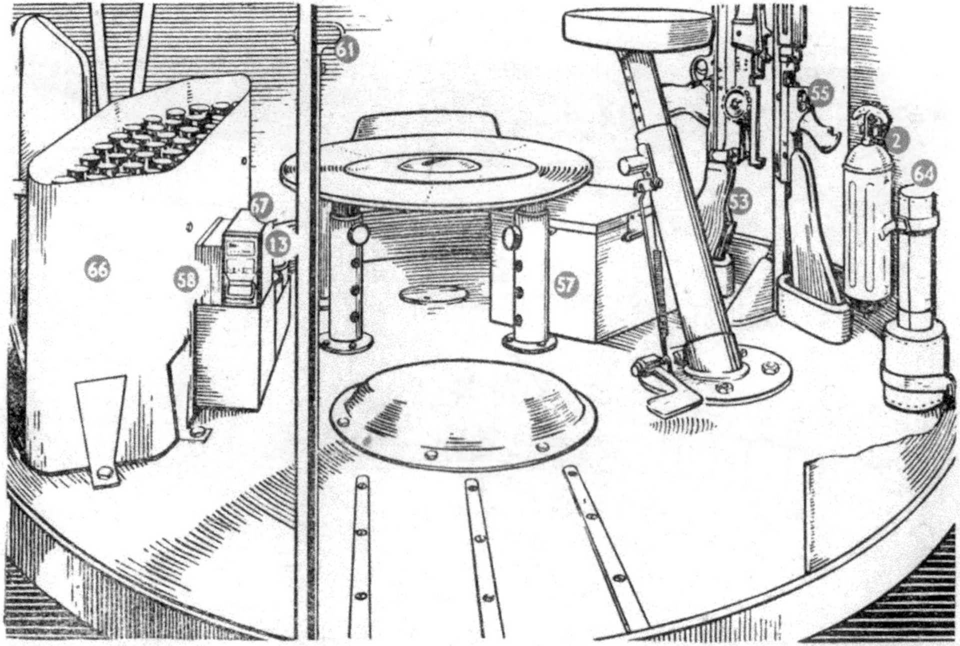

Fig. G. Churchill I and II. Turret platform. Churchill 2-pdr.

39

Fig. **H**. *Churchill I and II. Outside of vehicle. Churchill 2-pdr.*

STOWAGE—6-PDR.
(Churchill III and IV)
Illustrated on Plates I to S—pages 48 *to* 58.

The following is a complete list of the stowage items carried by the Churchill III and Churchill IV. The numbers in column 1 are the numbers by which the items are identified on the accompanying illustrations. Columns 2 and 3 list, respectively, the articles carried and the number of each supplied. Column 4 contains the reference letters of the illustrations on which the various items can be found. Drawings prepared for an earlier edition of the handbook have been utilised for this issue, necessitating omissions to the numbers in column 1.

VEHICLE EQUIPMENT

Item No.	Description	Number Carried	Plate Ref.
1	Fire extinguisher, CO_2—7 lb. bottle	2	K. L.
2	Fire extinguisher, Pyrene tetra-chloride type—1 quart ...	2	J. O.
2a	Fire extinguisher—methyl bromide	2	P.III. S.IV
3	Water tanks—drinking ...	2	J. L.
4	Greatcoats and camouflage net bin :—		P.III. S.IV
	Camouflage net for vehicle, 35 ft. by 15 ft.	1	
	3-piece waterproof cover for vehicle	1	
	Tent poles, 18 ins.	2	
	Tent pegs	4	
	Hemp rope, 20 ft.	1	
	Matchet (15 ins.) in case (see also No. 24, Fig. J.) ...	1	
	Greatcoats	5	
	Strips and disc, ground/air communication, per 10 vehicles	1 set	
5	Flag bag, with 3 signalling flags (1 set)	1	P.III. S.IV

41

STOWAGE—6-PDR.—continued

Item No.	Description	Number Carried	Plate Ref.
6	Turret headsets (microphone and receiver headgear No. 1 ; includes one carried as spare in signal satchel with sling)	4	N.III. R.IV
7	Hull headsets (microphone and receiver headgear No. 2, in bag ; includes one carried as spare in signal satchel with sling)	3	I. J.
8	Inspection lamp	1	I.
9	First aid outfit for tanks and armoured cars (packed) ...	1 box	J.
10	Portable cooker, No. 2 complete	1	L.
11	Miscellaneous bin :—		J.
	Muzzle cover—Bren M.G.	1	
	Cover—Thompson sub. M.G.	2	
	Pack—spares and tools— Besa	1	
	Gloves—wiring	2 prs.	
	Biscuit, 10 oz. ration ...	15 tins	
	Rations, No. 3. 5 men— 1 day (packed)	3 boxes	
	Water bottles	5	
	Muzzle cover—Besa med. M.G.	2	
	Muzzle cover—6-pdr. ...	1	
	Cleaning brush, 11 in. ...	1	
	Anti-gas ointment, tins of 8 tubes (see also No. 15, Fig. M.III or Q.IV.) ...	2	
	Haversacks—W.D. 37 Patt.	4	
12	Haversack—W.D. 37 Patt. ...	1	I.
	First aid outfit, small	1 box	S.
14	Bleach powder, 2 lb.	1 tin	N.III. R.IV
15	Anti-gas ointment, tin of 8 tubes (see also No. 11, Fig. J)	1	M.III. Q.IV

42

STOWAGE—6-PDR.—continued

Item No.	Description	Number Carried	Plate Ref.
16	Anti-dim compound, No. 2 (with flannelette)	1 jar	N.III. R.IV
17	Shovel, G.S.	2	P.III. S.IV
18	Pickaxe with helve	1	P.III. S.IV
19	Crowbar, 5 ft.	1	P.III. S.IV
20	Sledge hammer (10 lbs.) with handle	1	P.III. S.IV
22	Recognition signals—tank/air	1	N.III. R.IV
23	Ground sheets, Mk. VIII ...	5	I.
24	Matchet (15 ins.) in case (see also No. 4, Fig. P.III or S.IV.)	1	J.
25	Canvas bucket, Mk. V ...	1	I.
	Map board, G.S. No. 2, Mk. 1	1	R.
27	Wire cutters, folding, Mk. I (in frog)	1	I.
28	Hellesen hand lamp	2	L. N.III. R.IV
29	Wallet for commander ...	1	M.III. R.IV
30	Binoculars, prismatic	1	N.III. R.IV
31	Waterproof suits	2	L.
32	Suit—anti-gas	1	L.
33	Breech cover—6-pdr.	1	L.
34	Brush, bass hand,Mk. I ...	1	L.
35	Anti-gas cape and gloves ...	5	I. L.
36	Instruction book and tool lists	1	I.
37	Log book (Army Book AB.413)	1	I.
38	Hawser for towing, 15 ft. ...	2	P.III. S.IV
39	Packing blocks for jack (wood)	2	P.III. S.IV
40	Auxiliary battery charging set	1	J.
41	Oil can, $\frac{1}{2}$-pt., with angle spout	1	I.
42	Oil can, 1 gallon, Mk. II/L ...	1	K.
43	Water cans, 2-gallon	4	P.III. S.IV
45	Cocking lanyard, No. 4, Mk. I	1	M.III. Q.IV

EQUIPMENT SPARES

46	Prisms, object, Vickers' tank periscope.	12	J. M.III. N.III. Q.IV. R.IV

STOWAGE—6-PDR.—continued

Item No.	Description	Number Carried	Plate Ref.
47	Cleaning brush—prism ...	3	J. M.III. N.III. Q.IV. R.IV
48	Vision door triplex unit ...	2	I.
49	Spare valves case	1	N.III. R.IV
	Wireless valves. (See Parts Tables for details) ...	15	
50	W.T. spare parts case No. 5c	1	N.III. R.IV
	Bulbs, F., 12 v. 2.4 w. ...	4	
	W.T. key and plug, No. 9 ...	1	
	Rotary transformer brushes (H.T.), No. 4	4	
	Rotary transformer brushes (L.T.), No. 18	2	
	Fuses (radio), 250 m/a ...	12	
	Holders, No. 1 caps ...	2	
	Adjuster screws	6	
51	Main wireless aerial	1	J.
52	Troop set wireless aerial ...	2	N.III. R.IV

VEHICLE TOOLS

53	Vehicle tools, set (see Schedule of Tools for details) ...	1	I.
54	Hammer, engineer's, 2 lb. (Part of No. 53)	1	I.
55	Hose—bleeding Lockheed system	1	I.
56	Container—bleeding Lockheed fluid	1	I.
59	Tecalemit compressor, Junior No. 2, with ball swivel nozzle, type B.S.42	1	J.

VEHICLE SPARES

62	Spare bulb container	1	I.
	Spare side lamp bulb ...		

STOWAGE—6-PDR.—continued

Item No.	Description	Number Carried	Plate Ref.
	Spare head lamp bulb ...	1	
	Spare U.V. lamp bulb ...	1	
63	Idler adjusting packing ...	70	J.
		(Less those in use)	
64	Track link (with 1 in. dia. pin)	2	P.III. S.IV
	Track link pin, includes 4 in bag, (see No. 65, Fig. L.)	6	
	Track link pin retainer. With vehicle tools (see No. 53, Fig. I.)	6	
	Track link pin retainer lock. With vehicle tools (see No. 53, Fig. I.)	12	
	or		
	Track link (with 1¼ in. dia. ·pin)	2	
	Track link pin (Service) (includes 4 in bag, see No. 65, Fig. L.)	6	
65	Bag, spare track pins, No. 1, containing 4 spare pins ...	1	L.

ARMAMENT

66	M.G. Bren .303 Mk. I or Mk. II	1	O.
68	Thompson sub-machine gun	2	J. O.
69	Signal pistol No. 1, Mk. III or Mk. IV	1	N.III. R.IV

ARMAMENT TOOLS

70	Piasaba bin :—		O.
	Bristle cleaner, 6-pdr. ...	1	
	Sponge cap, 6-pdr.	1	
	Brush, cylinder rod ...	2	
	Cleaning rod—Bren cylinder	1	
	Protector, object glass ; in case. Spares for telescope	6	

STOWAGE—6-PDR.—continued

Item No.	Description	Number Carried	Plate Ref.
	Wire cutters, folding, Mk. I (in frog)	1	
72	Wallet—Bren .303 M.G. Mk. I spares	1	L.
73	Gun tool bin :—		K.
	Tools and spares, etc., 6-pdr. (see Parts Tables for details)	1	
	Cleaning rod—Bren cylinder	1	
74	Cotton waste	1 bdle.	N.III. R.IV
75	Oil can—recoil replenishment ..	1	M.III. Q.IV
76	Besa spares bin :—		J. M.III.
	Clearing plugs—Besa med. M.G., Mk. I	4	R.IV
	Oil can, M.G., Mk. II ...	1	
77	Cleaning rod—.303 M.G., Mk. IIb or Mk. IV	1	O.
77a	Cleaning rod—.303 M.G., Mk. IIb or Mk. I	1	M.III. Q.IV. R.IV
78	Cleaning brush—2 in. bomb thrower	1	M.III. Q.IV
79	Grease, M.G. Mk. I	1 can	M.III. Q.IV
80	Case and striker—6-pdr. ...	1	N.III. R.IV
81	Sighting telescope No. 33 in case No. 10 (optional) ...	1	O.
	Sighting telescope No. 30 in case No. 6 (optional) ...	1	O.
	Sighting telescope No. 39 in case (optional)	1	O.

AMMUNITION

Item No.	Description	Number Carried	Plate Ref.
82	Cartridge, 6-pdr., Q.F., anti-tank	85	K. L. O.
83	S.A.H.29, Mk. I/L, expendable (optional)	31 boxes	J. K. L. M.
	Belt, Besa med. M.G., Mk. I or II (optional)	31 boxes	N.III. R.IV

STOWAGE—6-PDR.—continued

Item No.	Description	Number Carried	Plate Ref.
84	Thompson sub-machine gun. (One box in position on forward gun) 20 rounds per box	42 boxes	J. M.III. Q.IV
85	Bren, .303 M.G. No. 2, Mk. I	6 drums	L. N.III. R.IV
86	Bomb, M.L. smoke, 2 in. mortar Mk. I	30	M.III. Q.IV
87	Hand grenade (Mills) ...	12	N.III. R.IV
	Grenade, W.P. Smoke (optional)	12	
88	Cartridge for signal pistol ...	12	N.III. R.IV

The following items are stowed loose at crew's discretion :—

Cover, bomb thrower ...	1
Blankets	5
Funnel—collapsible fuel ...	1
Filter, collapsible fuel funnel	1
Cushion seat—spare ...	1
Stretcher, ambulance, Mk. II ; and slings	2

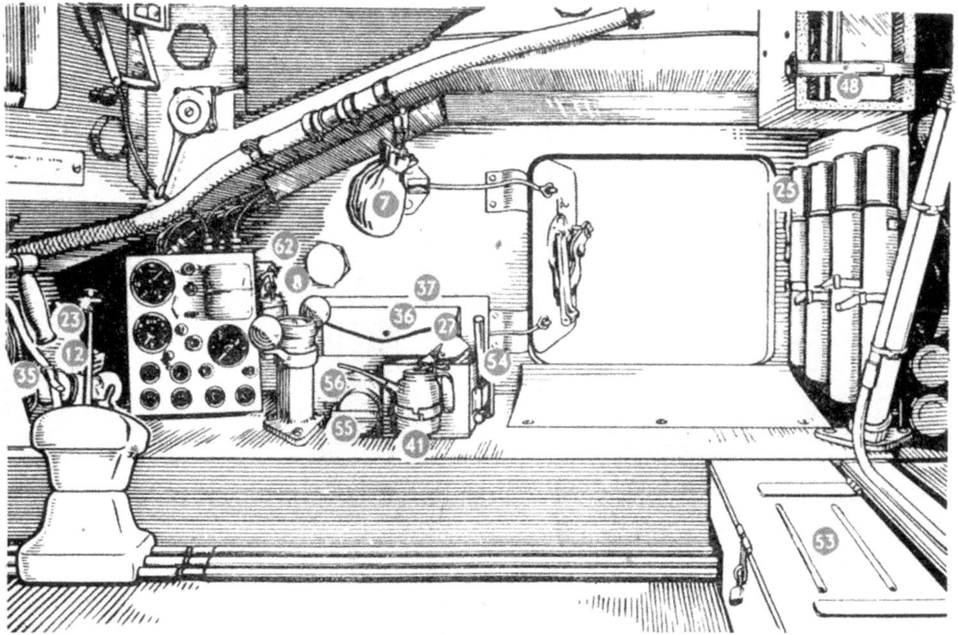

Fig. 1. Churchill III and IV. Driver's compartment—right-hand side.

Fig. J. *Churchill III and IV. Driver's compartment—left-hand side. Churchill 6-pdr.*

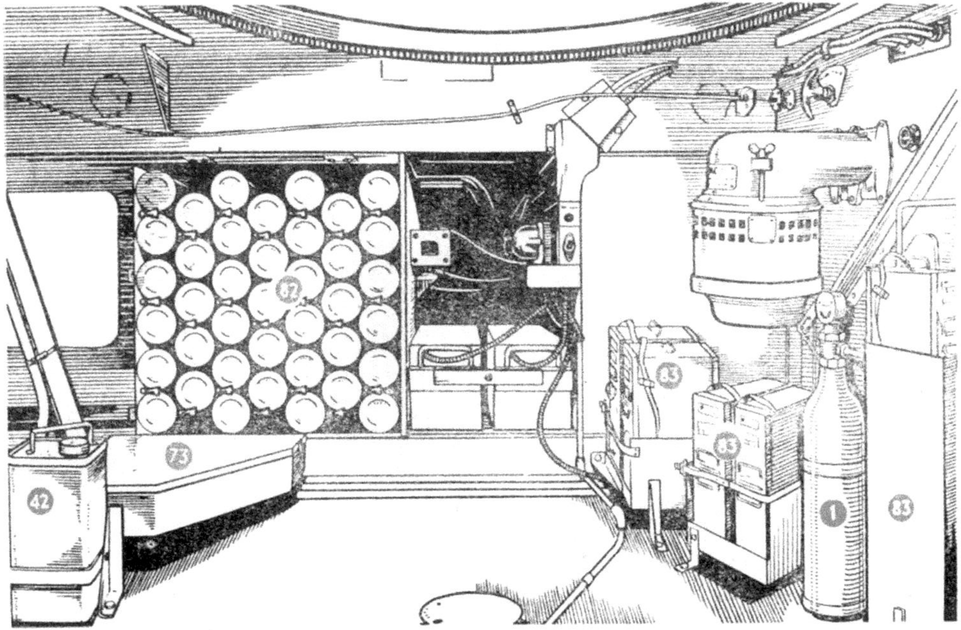

Fig. K. *Churchill III and IV.* Fighting compartment—right-hand side. *Churchill 6-pdr.*
Slight changes have been made since this illustration was produced. On current vehicles " two-stage " air cleaners are fitted and an accessories bin displaces items 83 in the rear corner, these items now being stowed as noted against Fig.L.

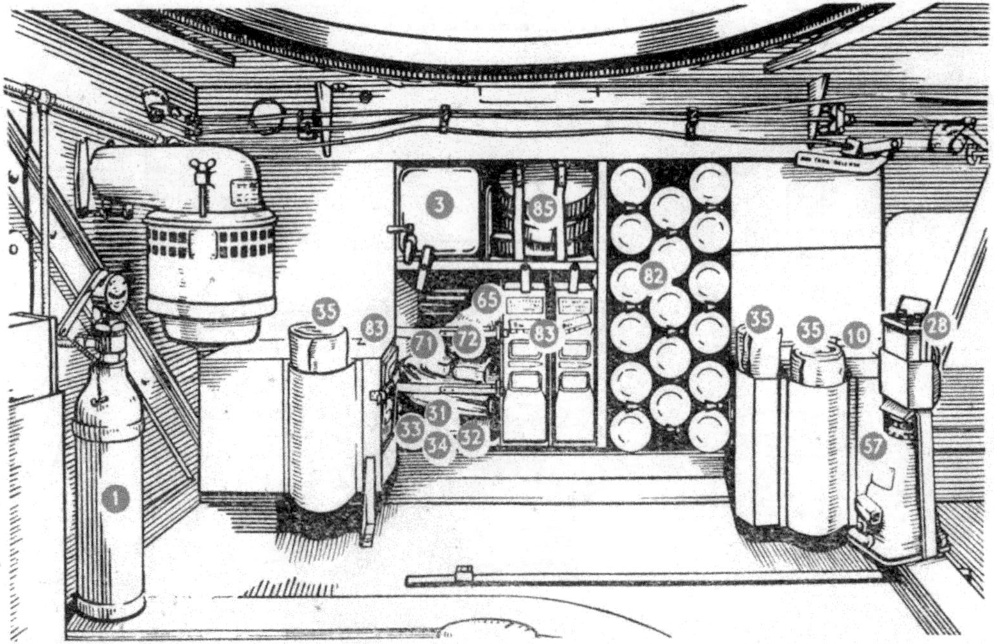

Fig. L. *Churchill III and IV. Fighting compartment—left-hand side. Churchill 6-pdr.*

Slight changes have been made since this illustration was produced. Current vehicles have "two-stage" air cleaners; items 31 to 35, 65 and 72 are stowed at crew's discretion in an accessories bin fitted in the rear corner; items 83 are now together at left-centre. Item 71 is deleted.

Fig. M. Churchill III. Turret interior—front half. Churchill 6-pdr.

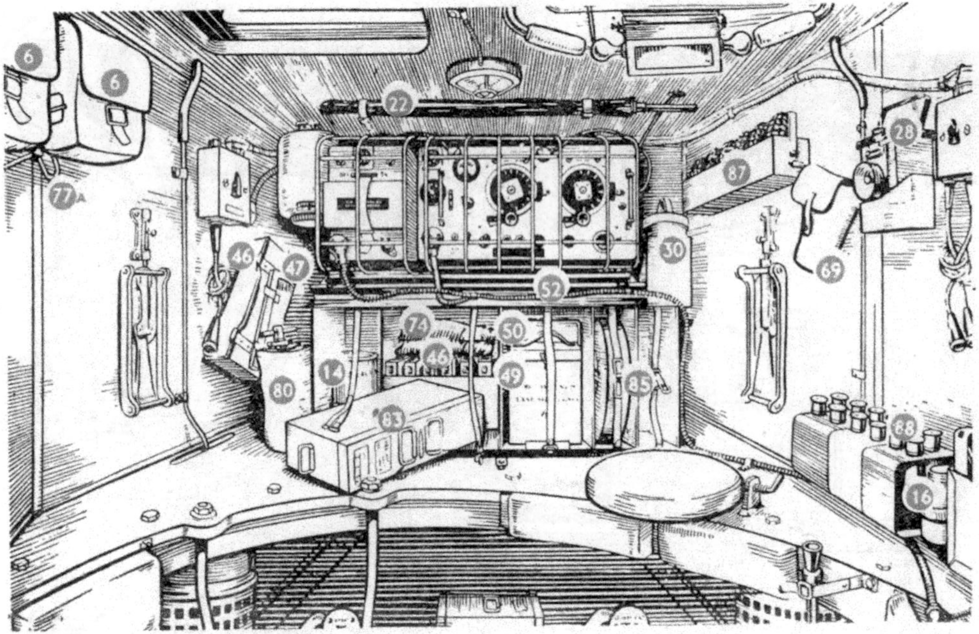

Fig. N. Churchill III. Turret interior—rear half. Churchill 6-pdr.

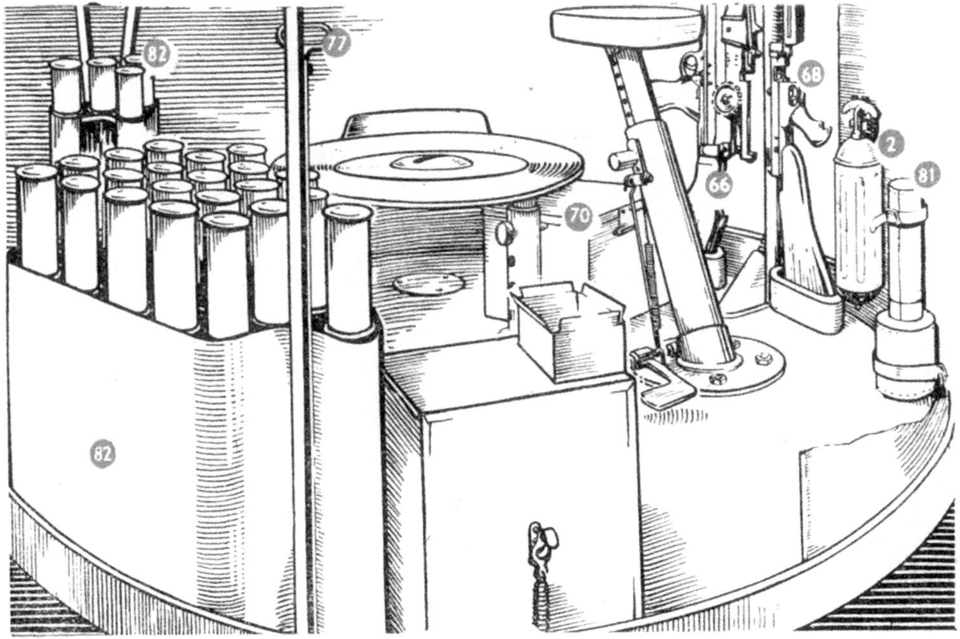

Fig. O. Churchill III and IV. Turret platform. Churchill 6-pdr.

Fig. P. *Churchill III. Outside of vehicle. Churchill 6-pdr.*

55

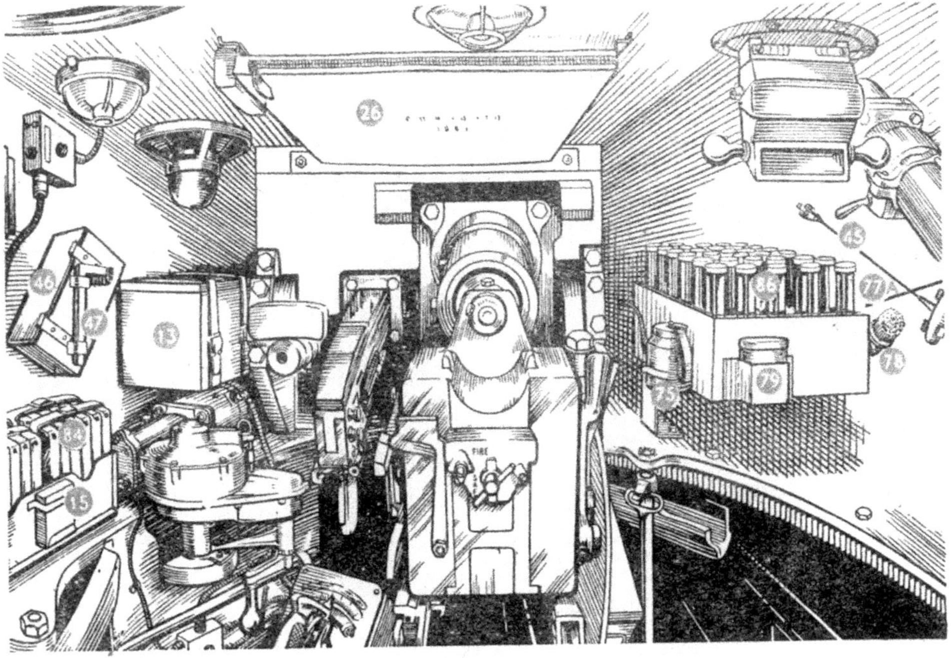

Fig. Q. *Churchill IV. Turret interior—front half.* *Churchill 6-pdr.*
Slight changes have been made since this illustration was produced. Items 13 and 26 are now *deleted* and two hand grenade boxes are added to the right of item 78.

Fig. R. Churchill IV. Turret interior—rear half. Churchill 6-pdr.

Fig. S. *Churchill IV. Outside of vehicle. Churchill 6-pdr.*
Slight changes have been made since this illustration was produced. Items 39 and 58 are deleted and a small First Aid box is added at the rear.

DIMENSIONS AND CAPACITIES

Dimensions

Overall Length of Vehicle – – – –	25' 2"
Overall Width of Vehicle – – – –	10' 8"
Width without Air Louvres – – – –	9' 2"
Overall Height – – – – – –	8' 2"
Ground Clearance – – – – – –	1' 8"
Length of Track on Ground – – – –	12' 6"
Width across Tracks – – – – –	9' 1"

Capacities

Petrol (all Tanks) – – – –	182½ gallons approx.
Right-hand Tanks – – – –	75 gallons approx.
Left-hand Tanks – – – –	75 gallons approx.
Jettison Tank – – – –	32½ gallons approx.
Cooling System – – – –	26 gallons approx.
	(13 gallons each side)
Oil in Engine – – – –	11 gallons approx.
Oil in Gearbox—Dry Box – –	3 gallons
Refill after draining	2½ gallons
Oil in each Final Drive Unit – –	1¾ gallons
Oil in Air Compressor Sump – –	1½ pints

Turning Radii

First Speed – – – – – –	10.85 ft.
Second Speed – – – – – –	29.8 ft.
Third Speed – – – – – –	57.4 ft.
Fourth Speed – – – – – –	95.9 ft.

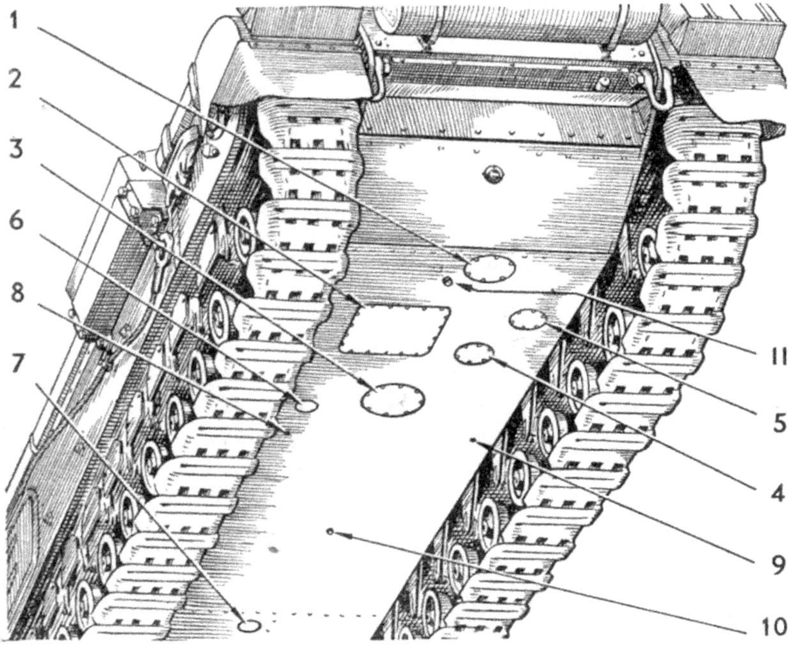

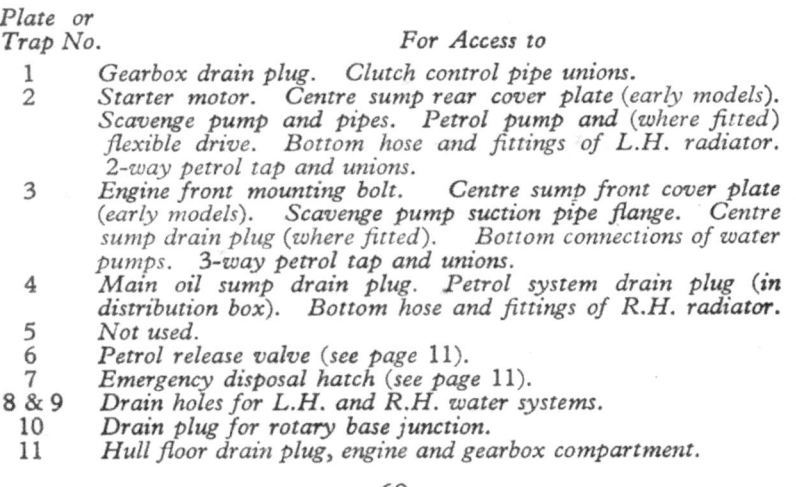

Fig. 16. *Inspection plates and traps in hull floor.*

Plate or Trap No.	For Access to
1	Gearbox drain plug. Clutch control pipe unions.
2	Starter motor. Centre sump rear cover plate (early models). Scavenge pump and pipes. Petrol pump and (where fitted) flexible drive. Bottom hose and fittings of L.H. radiator. 2-way petrol tap and unions.
3	Engine front mounting bolt. Centre sump front cover plate (early models). Scavenge pump suction pipe flange. Centre sump drain plug (where fitted). Bottom connections of water pumps. 3-way petrol tap and unions.
4	Main oil sump drain plug. Petrol system drain plug (**in** distribution box). Bottom hose and fittings of R.H. radiator.
5	Not used.
6	Petrol release valve (see page 11).
7	Emergency disposal hatch (see page 11).
8 & 9	Drain holes for L.H. and R.H. water systems.
10	Drain plug for rotary base junction.
11	Hull floor drain plug, engine and gearbox compartment.

MAINTENANCE

An athlete is kept at the top of his form by correct feeding and regular exercise. A tank is kept in fighting trim by correct lubrication and regular adjustments. Both may fail at the critical moment if these preliminaries are neglected—but there the comparison ends.

The athlete can fall out of a race with nothing more serious than a slight loss of reputation. The fighting vehicle dare not fail in the middle of an action.

Maintenance, therefore, is of vital importance. It is a wearisome job, a repetition time and time again of the same routine. But it is the surest, safest, wisest form of insurance known to mechanical warfare.

In the following pages the maintenance routine for the Churchill Tank is detailed under periods showing when the respective operations should be carried out. " Lubrication " items are printed in ordinary type, and " Inspections and Adjustments " are shown in capital letters. A lubrication chart is folded inside the back cover.

Make up your mind to follow these instructions conscientiously. Remember, maintenance is meaningless without regularity.

OILS AND GREASE

The correct grades of oil and grease are specified in this handbook and in the instruction book. Alternatives are *not* suitable and should not be used.

For the engine, and for all points requiring engine oil, use 10 H.D.

For the gearbox and all points requiring gear oil, use C.600. (This includes all *pressure nipples* lubricated with the oil gun, and is the only lubricant used in the gun).

For all *screw-down greasers*, use Grease No. 3 (high melting point).

For the Lockheed systems use Lockheed Racing Green or Hydraulic Brake Fluid No. 4. Never use oil (which causes rapid deterioration of the rubber pistons) or an incorrect brake fluid (which may vaporise at the high temperatures generated and thus render the brakes inoperative).

61

DAILY ROUTINE

1. Check engine oil level. Top up as required with engine oil (10HD). The dip-stick is under (or next to) the filler, and the oil should be replenished up to the " full " mark. (The " low " mark indicates the danger level). The vehicle should be on level ground. 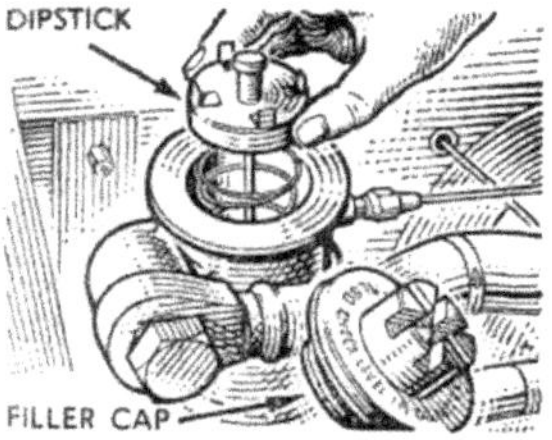
Run engine for 10 minutes at 1,000 r.p.m., switch off, wait for two minutes and check oil level again, with dipstick perfectly clean. Add oil if necessary to bring level *exactly* to the " full " mark.
(*Job No. A.1 in Instruction Book*)

2. Check petrol tank levels. Do not fill main tanks above $4\frac{1}{4}$ in. from top of filler. The auxiliary tank should be filled to the top. Petrol not below 75 Octane must be used. Check also the operation of the petrol controls.
(*Job No. A.1 in Instruction Book*)

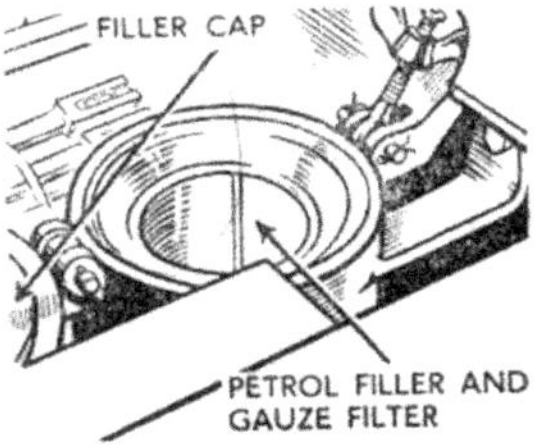

3. Check water levels—one filler cap on each side of engine compartment at the front. Securely fasten both caps after checking as the system operates under pressure.
(*Job No. A.1 in Instruction Book*)

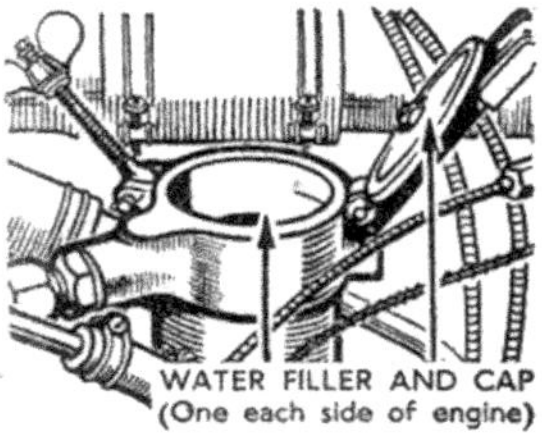

4. CHECK CLUTCH OPERATION AT END OF DAY'S RUN FOR CORRECT CLEARANCE AND COMPLETE DISENGAGEMENT, AND ADJUST IF NECESSARY.
(*Job No. A.10 in Instruction Book*)

LUBRICATION OPERATIONS ARE IN ORDINARY TYPE ;

DAILY ROUTINE—continued

5. INSPECT OIL AND FUEL PIPES FOR LEAKAGE OR FRACTURE AT END OF DAY'S RUN.

6. Lubricate bogie axles and fulcrum shafts (22 nipples each) with gear oil (C.600) using pressure gun. Inject oil in bogie axles until surplus flows from vent on rear side of axle shaft bracket, and in fulcrum shafts until oil exudes round the boss of the shaft.

NOTE. Every 50 *miles* is sufficient when *daily* mileage is less than 50.

(*Job No. A.2 in Instruction Book*)

FULCRUM SHAFT OIL NIPPLE

BOGIE AXLE OIL NIPPLE

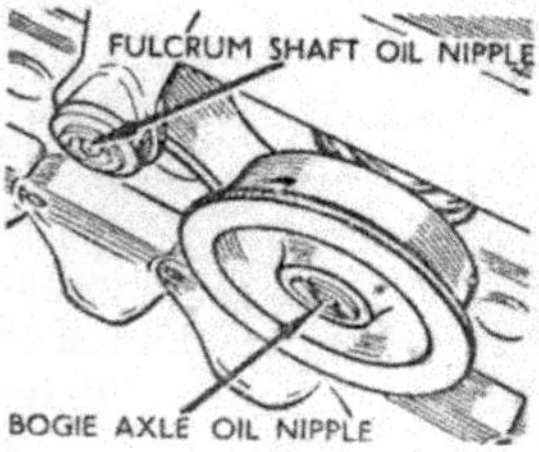

7. INSPECT TRACK SOLE PLATES FOR CRACKS, AND INSPECT FOR LOOSE TRACK PIN RETAINERS. REPORT ANY DEFECTS.

8. INSPECT BOLTS ON BOGIE BRACKET TIE PLATES, AND TIGHTEN IF NECESSARY.

NOTE.—THE REAR BOLT ON EACH PLATE IS ALLOWED A SMALL END CLEARANCE, BUT THE FRONT BOLT SHOULD CLAMP THE TIE PLATE FIRMLY. BOTH NUTS ARE SECURED BY LOCK-NUTS.

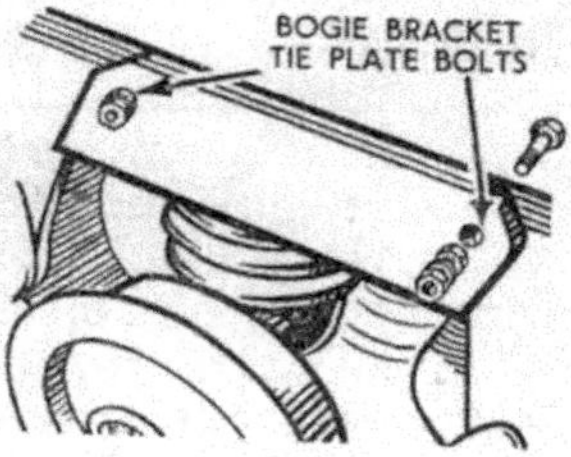

BOGIE BRACKET TIE PLATE BOLTS

9. Check oil level in compressor. Top up as required with engine oil (10 H.D.). Fill to top of filler hole.

(*Job No. A.2 in Instruction Book*)

OIL LEVEL AND FILLER

DRAIN PLUG

INSPECTIONS AND ADJUSTMENTS IN CAPITAL LETTERS

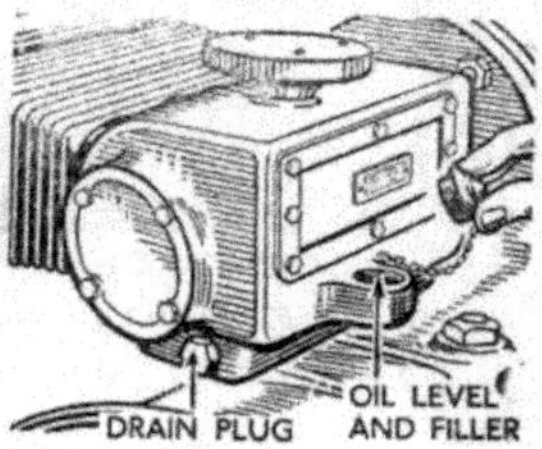

DAILY ROUTINE—continued

10. CHECK OPERATION OF ELECTRICAL EQUIPMENT. MAKE SURE THAT THE MAIN DYNAMO IS CHARGING CORRECTLY. CHECK OPERATION OF TURRET TRAVERSE GEAR, MASTER SWITCH, IGNITION AND PETROL WARNING LIGHTS.

11. Lubricate hinges on escape hatches and revolver ports, and mechanism of vision port with engine oil (10 H.D.). Also hinges of loading doors and vision port if pressure nipples are not fitted. Lubricate edges of loading doors, vision port, revolver ports and escape hatches with gear oil (C.600). (*Job No. A.2 in Instruction Book*)

See item 24 on page 71 (250 miles) for hinges fitted with pressure nipples.

12. Lubricate gun depression roller shaft (on elevating bracket under gun mounting). One hole each end (C.600). (*Job No. A.2 in Instruction Book*)

13. Check oil level in auxiliary generator engine (whenever generator has been in use). Top up as required with engine oil (10 H.D.). Fill to bottom thread of filler plug. (*Job No. A.2 in Instruction Book*)

AUXILIARY GENERATOR
ENGINE OIL LEVEL
AND FILLER PLUG

DRAIN PLUG

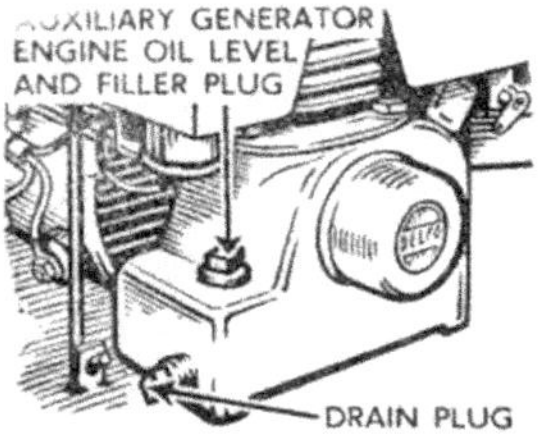

LUBRICATION OPERATIONS ARE IN ORDINARY TYPE ;

EFFECTS OF OPERATING CONDITIONS

The following extra routine must be carried out at the stated intervals when operating in dusty conditions.

DAILY

On early vehicles wash out air cleaner elements and casings and refill to level mark with engine oil (10 H.D.).

Refer to illustration on page 72 (item 2—upper).

Later vehicles have " two-stage " air cleaners. Remove the bottom dust containers and empty them. Before replacing make sure that the dust ejection slots are free and that no oil drips into the centrifugal conical pans.

Refer to illustration on page 72 (item 2—lower).

(*Job No. A.3 in Instruction Book*)

REMOVE AIR INLET LOUVRES AND CLEAN AIR PASSAGES IN RADIATOR CORES.

IF POSSIBLE, THE AIR PASSAGES SHOULD BE BLOWN OUT WITH COMPRESSED AIR FROM THE CENTRE OF THE VEHICLE OUTWARDS.

THIS WILL NOT BE NECESSARY ON VEHICLES FITTED WITH FULL-LENGTH MUDGUARDS AND UPTURNED LOUVRES.

EVERY 250 MILES

WASH FILTER CLOTH OF AIR COMPRESSOR INLET.

(*Job No. B.21 in Instruction Book*)

Refer to illustration on page 75 (item 16).

INSPECTIONS AND ADJUSTMENTS IN CAPITAL LETTERS

EVERY 250 MILES

(Or WEEKLY when the weekly mileage is less than 250)

1. REMOVE AND EMPTY THE BOTTOM DUST CONTAINERS ON THE "TWO-STAGE" AIR CLEANERS FITTED TO LATER VEHICLES. BEFORE REPLACING THEM, MAKE SURE THAT THE DUST EJECTION SLOTS ARE FREE AND THAT NO OIL DRIPS INTO THE CENTRIFUGAL CONICAL PANS.

Refer to illustration on page 72 (item 2—lower).

2. CHECK TENSION OF WATER PUMP DRIVING BELTS AND ADJUST IF NECESSARY.

(Job No. A.6 in Instruction Book)

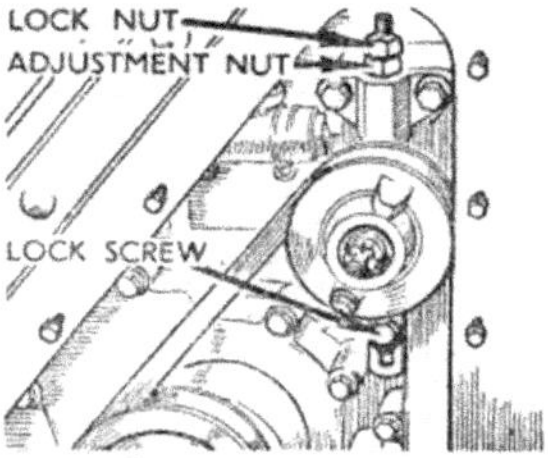

3. Lubricate throttle control rod joints with engine oil (10 H.D.). *(Job No. A.2 in Instruction Book)*

4. CHECK THROTTLE CONTROL ROD NUTS FOR TIGHTNESS.

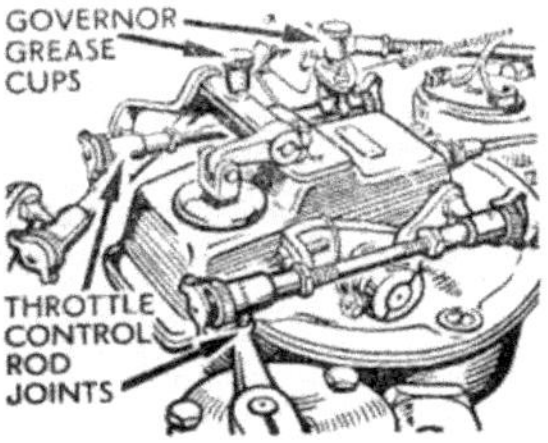

5. CHECK TENSION OF MAIN DYNAMO DRIVING BELT AND ADJUST IF NECESSARY. *(Job No. A.6 in Instruction Book)*

LUBRICATION OPERATIONS ARE IN ORDINARY TYPE;

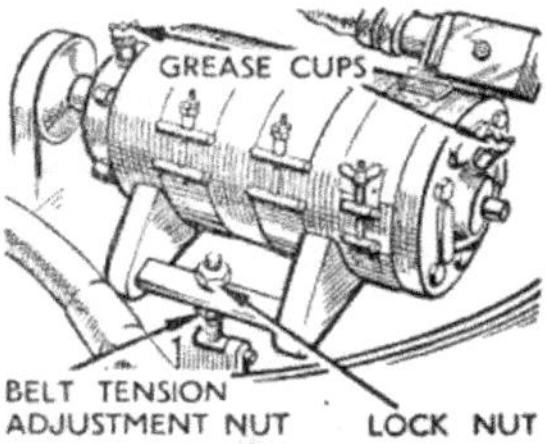

EVERY 250 MILES—continued

6. Examine level of electrolyte in batteries and top up if required. The two 6-volt batteries are fitted on the floor of the battery recess. *Check more frequently in exceptionally hot conditions.*

7. CHECK BATTERY CONNECTIONS FOR TIGHTNESS. CLEAN TERMINALS AND SMEAR WITH VASELINE.

---

8. Check gearbox oil level of turret traverse gear. Top up if necessary with 10 H.D. to level of filler plug.

(*Job No. A.2 in Instruction Book*)

TRAVERSE GEARBOX OIL FILLER

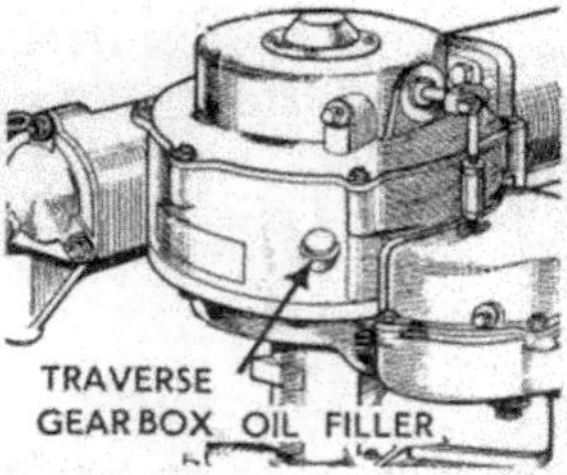

9. Lubricate three nipples of clutch throw-out mechanism with gear oil (C.600).

(*Job No. A.2 in Instruction Book*)

CLUTCH THROW-OUT OIL NIPPLES

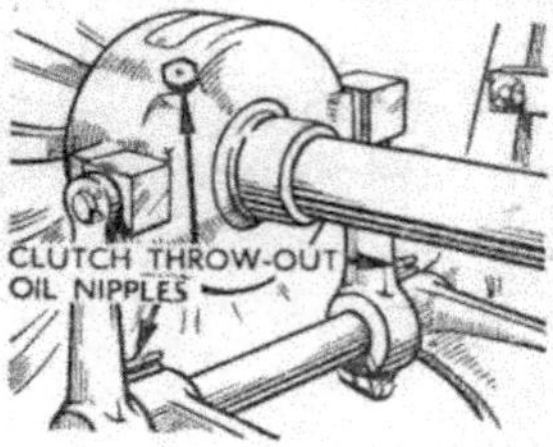

10. Lubricate clevis joints of clutch servo motor with engine oil (10 H.D.).

(*Job No. A.2 in Instruction Book*)

CLEVIS JOINTS

INSPECTIONS AND ADJUSTMENTS IN CAPITAL LETTERS

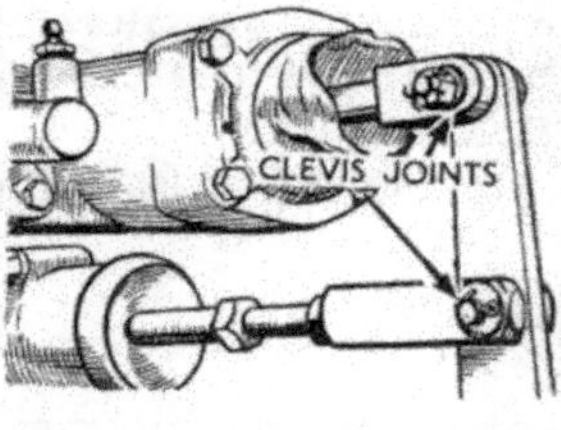

EVERY 250 MILES—continued

11. CHECK TENSION OF TURRET GENERATOR DRIVING BELT AND ADJUST IF NECESSARY.

(*Job No. A.6 in Instruction Book*)

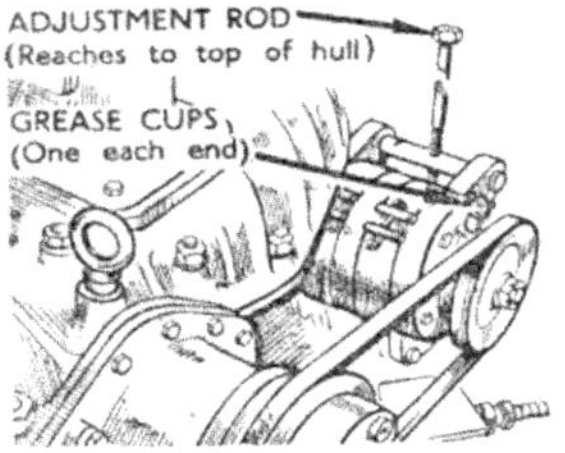

12. Top up fluid level in brake fluid reservoir, if required, *with Lockheed Hydraulic Racing Green or Hydraulic Brake Fluid No. 4.* The filler plug is situated under the driver's escape hatch. The level plug is fitted in the pipe about halfway between the filler plug and the reservoir.

(*Job No. A.2 in Instruction Book*)

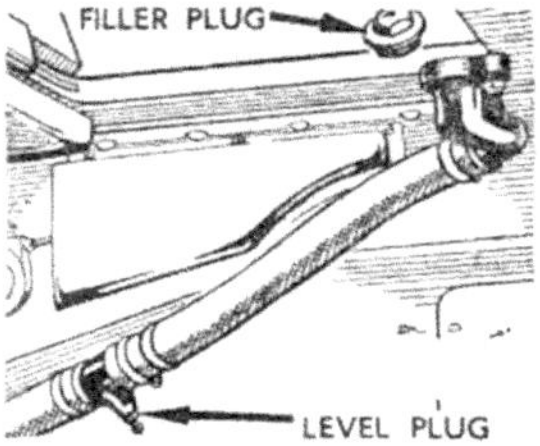

13. Lubricate bracket bearings for speedometer drive with engine oil (10 H.D.). Not on vehicles fitted with fixed pulley.

(*Job No. A.2 in Instruction Book*)

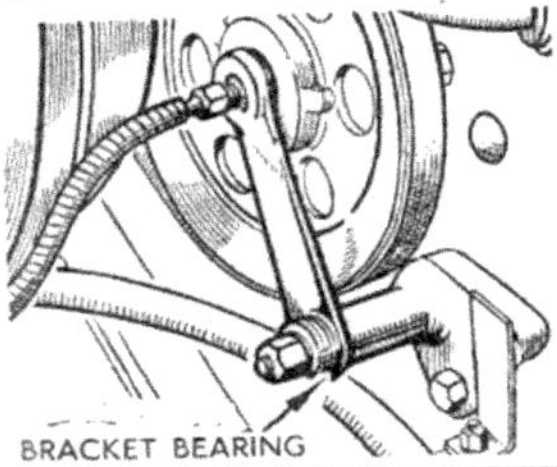

14. Lubricate control rod joints, actuating levers and sliding rods of change speed mechanism with engine oil (10 H.D.). Also gate mechanism and rods in gear change lever bracket. On five-speed gearbox lubricate the bell crank pivot housing with gear oil (C.600).

(*Job No. A.2 in Instruction Book*)

LUBRICATION OPERATIONS ARE IN ORDINARY TYPE ;

EVERY 250 MILES—continued

15. Check gearbox oil level and top up as required with gear oil (C.600). Allow time for the oil to find its level before re-checking.

(*Job No. A.2 in Instruction Book*)

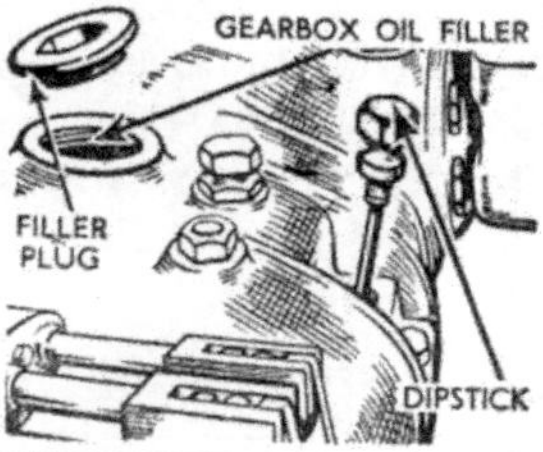

16. Lubricate two nipples on each periscope with C.600, using the pressure gun.
(*Job No. A.2 in Instruction Book*)

17. Lubricate clip and hinge pin of each periscope glass container with engine oil (10 H.D.).
(*Job No. A.2 in Instruction Book*)

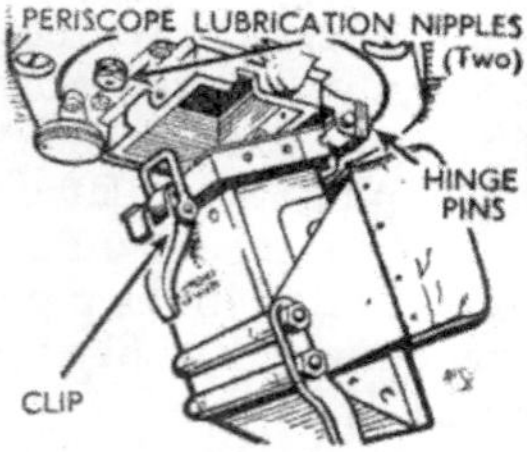

18. Lubricate gun trunnion bearings with engine oil (10 H.D.)—or with C.600 if pressure nipples are fitted.

Note that on later vehicles with front Besa gun a lubricator is fitted to the bottom trunnion of the No. 19 M.G. front Besa gimbal mounting (C.600).

(*Job No. A.2 in Instruction Book*)

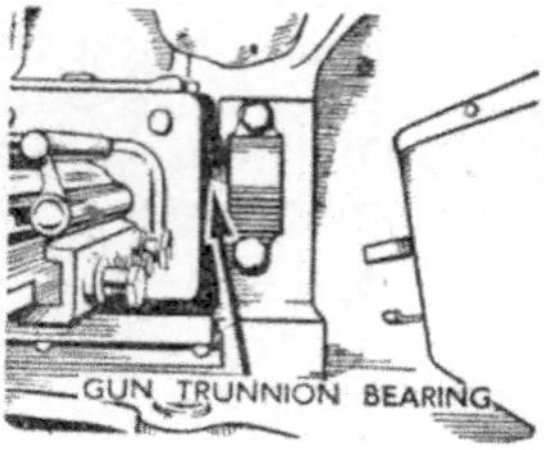

Upper illustration on right shows 2-Pdr. Gun Trunnion Bearing, Churchill I and II.

Lower illustration 6-Pdr. Gun Trunnion Bearing Churchill III and IV (2 nipples—one each side.)

INSPECTIONS AND ADJUSTMENTS IN CAPITAL LETTERS

EVERY 250 MILES—continued

19. Lubricate six nipples on turret race inner ring with gear oil (C.600). Traverse turret slowly and continue to lubricate until oil oozes out beneath the race *all round.*
(*Job No. A.2 in Instruction Book*)

20. CHECK FINAL DRIVE COUPLING BOLTS AND TIGHTEN IF NECESSARY.

FINAL DRIVE COUPLING BOLTS

21. Examine level in final drive assemblies and top up as required with gear oil (C.600). The filler plug in the final drive casing is reached through a hole in the hull side plate closed by a bolted on cover. Remove the cover, and rotate the final drive until the filler plug comes opposite the hole.
(*Job No. A.2 in Instruction Book*)

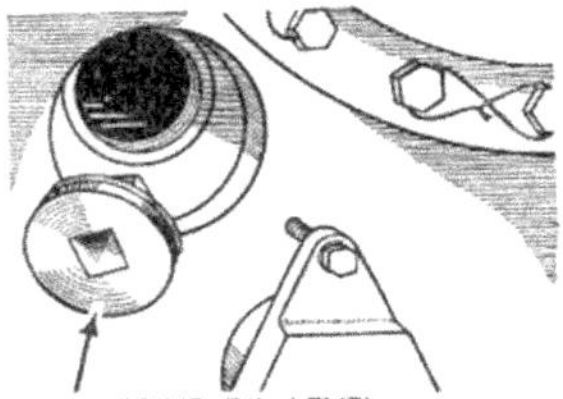

FINAL DRIVE OIL LEVEL AND FILLER PLUG

22. START AUXILIARY PETROL ELECTRIC GENERATOR AND CHECK FOR CORRECT OPERATION.

23. Lubricate auxiliary tank release mechanism at rear of hull with gear oil (C.600).
(*Job No. A.2 in Instruction Book*)

AUXILIARY TANK RELEASE MECHANISM

LUBRICATION OPERATIONS ARE IN ORDINARY TYPE ;

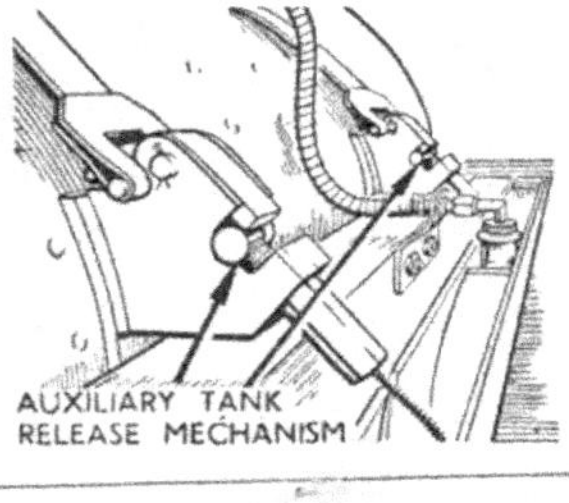

EVERY 250 MILES—continued

24. Lubricate hinges on loading doors and vision port with gear oil (C.600). Only on vehicles fitted with pressure nipples for this purpose.

(*Job No. A.2 in Instruction Book*)

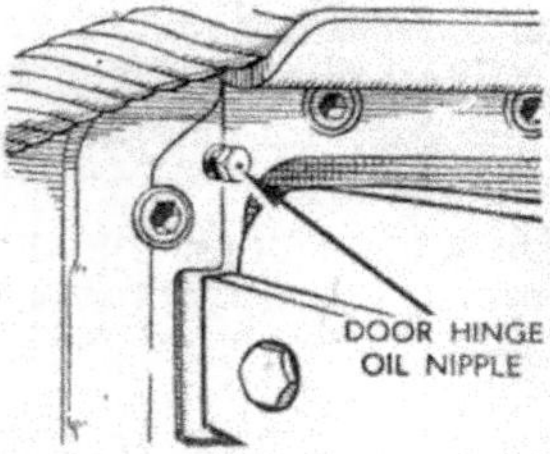

DOOR HINGE
OIL NIPPLE

25. Lubricate all moving parts of turret traverse handle (10 H.D.).

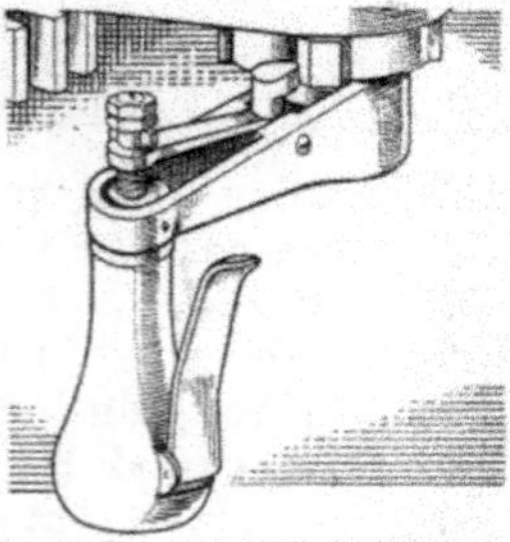

26. CHECK BOGIE ATTACHING BOLTS (88 PLACES) FOR TIGHTNESS.
(*Job No. A.17 in Instruction Book*)

27. REMOVE DRAIN PLUG FROM BASE OF ROTARY BASE JUNCTION BOX AND ALLOW ANY WATER TO DRAIN AWAY.

Position of drain plug shown in Fig. 16, page 60.

INSPECTIONS AND ADJUSTMENTS IN CAPITAL LETTERS

EVERY 500 MILES

(Or MONTHLY when the monthly mileage is less than 500)

1. Drain engine oil, renew A.C. oil filter elements, clean oil strainers, and refill engine with engine oil (10 H.D.).
The engine oil should be changed every 500 miles and NOT monthly if the monthly mileage is less than 500.
(Job No. A.5 in Instruction Book)

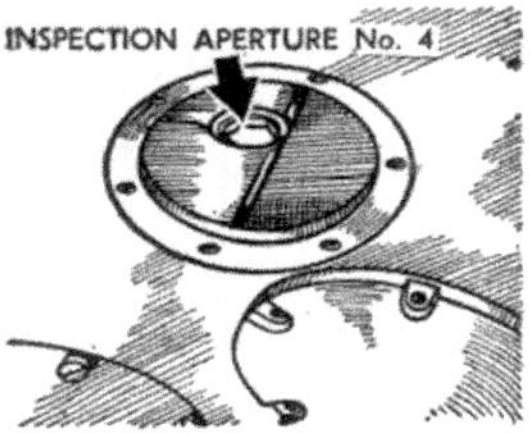

2. On early vehicles wash out air filter elements and casings and re-fill casings to level mark with engine oil (10 H.D.). There are two air filters, mounted on the engine front bulkheads.
On later vehicles "two-stage" air cleaners are fitted. On each of the two cleaners, remove the filter element, wash and drain. Wash out the oil pan and refill with engine oil (10 H.D.) to level mark, replacing empty compensator bowl when re-assembling. Examine the cork seal in the head and the neoprene seal in the shell. Tighten side wing nuts fully. Empty bottom dust container and ensure that dust ejection slots are free and that no oil drips into the centrifugal conical pan.
Note.—Do not tilt a cleaner excessively when detached and always remove the compensator when filling.
See special section—" Effects of Operating Conditions " on page 65.
(Job No. A.3 in Instruction Book)

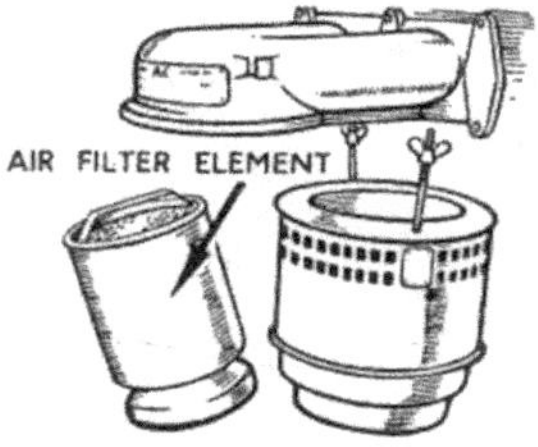

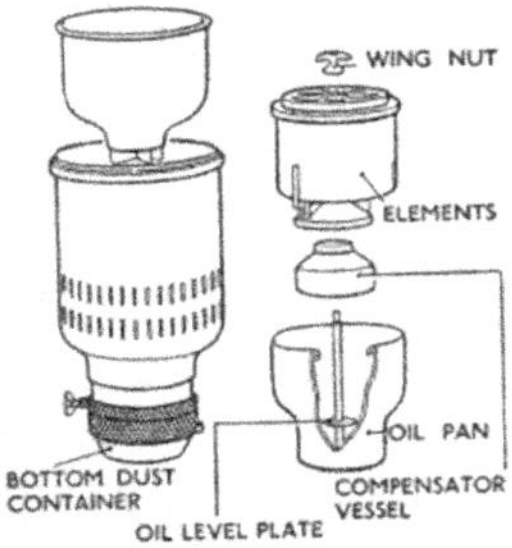

LUBRICATION OPERATIONS ARE IN ORDINARY TYPE ;

EVERY 500 MILES—continued

3. CLEAN CONTACT BREAKER POINTS AND RESET IF NECESSARY. GAP .010 TO .012 IN.

(*Job No. A.7 in Instruction Book*)

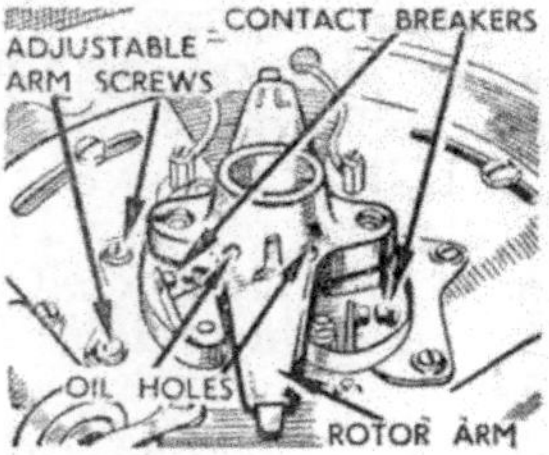

4. Screw down governor grease cups (2) one complete turn. If the grease cups need refilling, Grease No. 3 must be used.

Job No. A.2 in Instruction Book)

(*See illustration to item 3, page* 66).

5. CLEAN STRAINERS (2) IN PETROL PUMP BY REMOVING METAL FILTER BOWLS AND FLUSHING OUT. IT IS NOT NECESSARY TO REMOVE THE STRAINERS. (ACCESS THROUGH TRAP 2—SEE PAGE 60).

(*Job No. A.3 in Instruction Book*)

6. FLUSH OUT CARBURETTOR BOWLS AND CLEAN STRAINERS IN BANJO CONNECTIONS AT CARBURETTOR BOWLS (4).

(*Job No. A.4 in Instruction Book*)

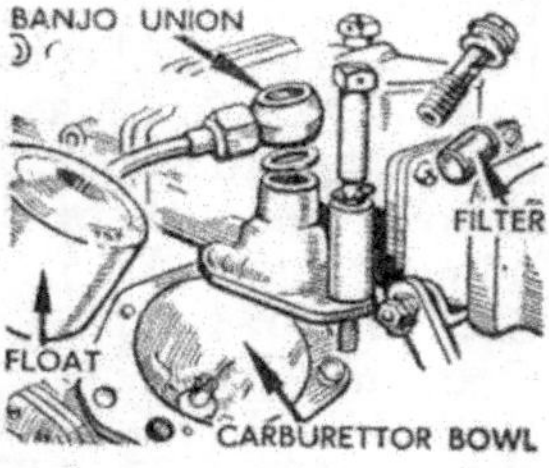

INSPECTIONS AND ADJUSTMENTS IN CAPITAL LETTERS

EVERY 500 MILES—continued

7. Screw down engine tachometer grease cup one complete turn. If the grease cup needs refilling, Grease No. 3 must be used.

(*Job No. A.2 in Instruction Book*)

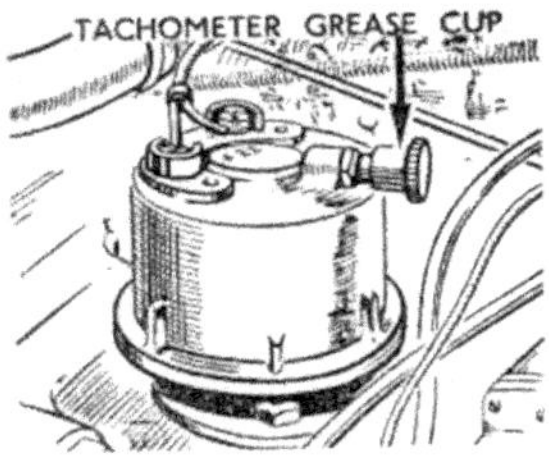

8. REMOVE PLUG FROM AIR COMPRESSOR OUTLET FILTER AND DRAIN OFF WATER.

(*Job No. A.15 in Instruction Book*)

9. EXAMINE UNLOADER VALVE ON THE AIR COMPRESSOR RESERVOIR; LAP VALVE SEATS IF NECESSARY WITH METAL POLISH.

(*Job No. B.21 in Instruction Book*)

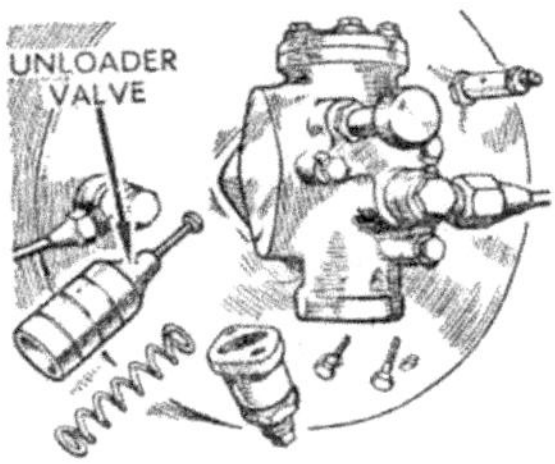

10. REMOVE AIR INLET LOUVRES AND CLEAN AIR PASSAGES IN RADIATOR CORES. IF POSSIBLE THE AIR PASSAGES SHOULD BE BLOWN OUT WITH COMPRESSED AIR FROM THE CENTRE OF THE VEHICLE OUTWARDS.

SEE SPECIAL SECTION " EFFECTS OF OPERATING CONDITIONS " ON PAGE 65.

LUBRICATION OPERATIONS ARE IN ORDINARY TYPE ;

EVERY 500 MILES—continued

11. Lubricate two nipples on steering servo cylinders with gear oil (C.600).

(*Job No. A.2 in Instruction Book*)

12. Refill oil cups (2) of steering servo cylinders with engine oil (10 H.D.).

(*Job No. A.2 in Instruction Book*)

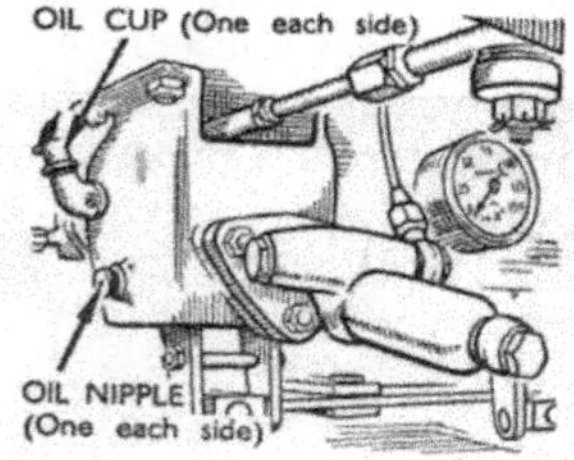

13. Lubricate pivots and ratchet release on hand-brake mechanism with engine oil (10 H.D.).

(*Job No. A.2 in Instruction Book*)

14. Drain oil from air compressor and refill with engine oil (10 H.D.). Fill to level of filler plug.

(*See illustration to item 9 page 63*).

(*Job No. A.2 in Instruction Book*)

15. REMOVE CYLINDER HEAD OF AIR COMPRESSOR AND RENEW INLET AND OUTLET DISC VALVES.

THIS MUST BE DONE AFTER EVERY 500 MILES—NOT MONTHLY IF THE MILEAGE IS LESS THAN 500.

(*Job No. B.21 in Instruction Book*)

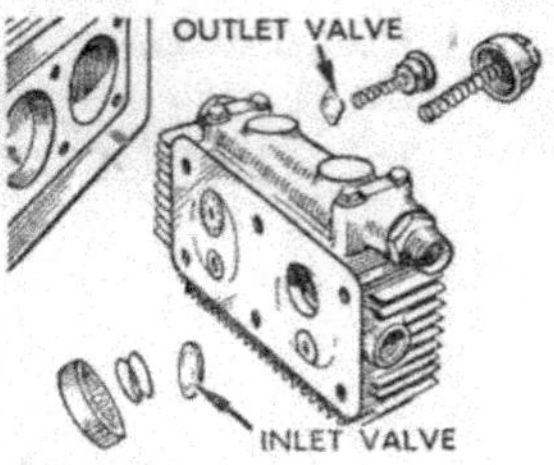

16. WASH FILTER CLOTH OF AIR COMPRESSOR INLET.

(NOTE. SEE SPECIAL SECTION " EFFECTS OF OPERATING CONDITIONS " ON PAGE 65).

(*Job No. B.21 in Instruction Book*)

INSPECTIONS AND ADJUSTMENTS IN CAPITAL LETTERS

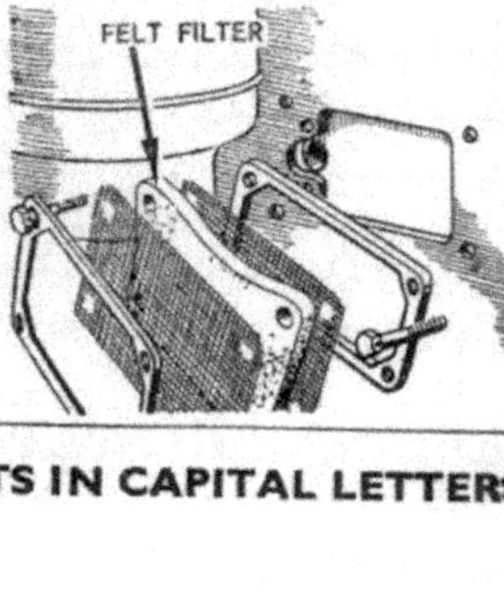

EVERY 500 MILES—continued

17. DRAIN PETROL DISTRIBUTION BOX AS FOLLOWS. TURN PETROL CONTROLS TO " OFF." REMOVE DRAIN PLUG (SEE PAGE 60). TURN ON PETROL FROM ONE OF THE TANKS TO FLUSH OUT THE BOX. TURN OFF PETROL AND REPLACE PLUG SECURELY AFTER FLUSHING.

(*Job No. A.3 in Instruction Book*)

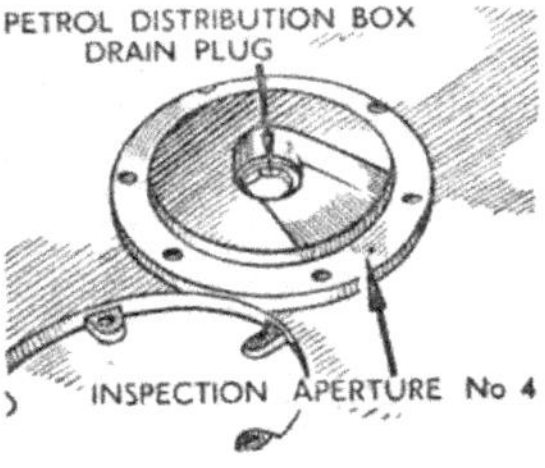

PETROL DISTRIBUTION BOX
DRAIN PLUG

INSPECTION APERTURE No 4

---

18. EXAMINE TIGHTNESS AND CLEANLINESS OF TERMINALS IN THE ROTARY BASE JUNCTION BOX.

---

19. Screw down main dynamo grease cups (if fitted) one complete turn. If the grease cups need refilling, Grease No. 3 must be used.

(*Job No. A.2 in Instruction Book*)

(*See illustration to item* 5, *page* 66).

---

20. CLEAN DISTRIBUTOR COVERS AND CHECK WIRING CONNECTIONS FOR TIGHTNESS.

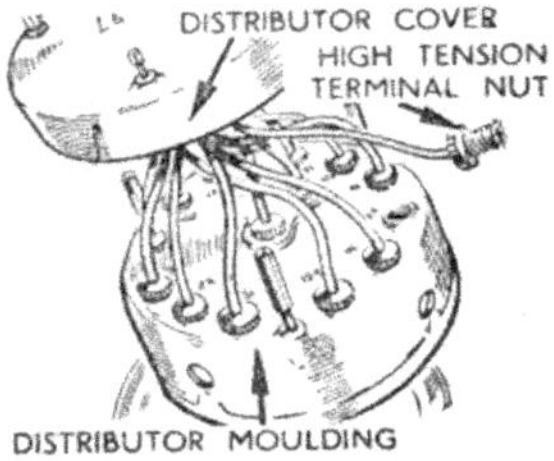

DISTRIBUTOR COVER
HIGH TENSION
TERMINAL NUT

DISTRIBUTOR MOULDING

---

21. Screw down turret generator grease cups (if fitted) one complete turn. If the grease cups need refilling *Grease No. 3 must be used.*

(*Job No. A.2 in Instruction Book*)

(*See illustration to item* 11, *page* 68).

LUBRICATION OPERATIONS ARE IN ORDINARY TYPE ;

76

EVERY 500 MILES—continued

22. Fill oil cup on starter motor with engine oil (10 H.D.). Access through Trap 2 (see page 60).

(*Job No. A.2 in Instruction Book*)

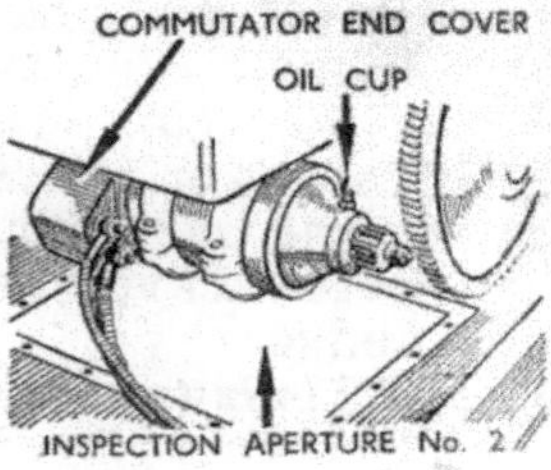

COMMUTATOR END COVER

OIL CUP

INSPECTION APERTURE No. 2

INSPECTIONS AND ADJUSTMENTS IN CAPITAL LETTERS

EVERY 1,000 MILES

1. EXAMINE BRUSH GEAR OF TURRET TRAVERSE MOTOR FOR WEAR AND CLEANLINESS.
(*Job No. A.*16 *in Instruction Book*)

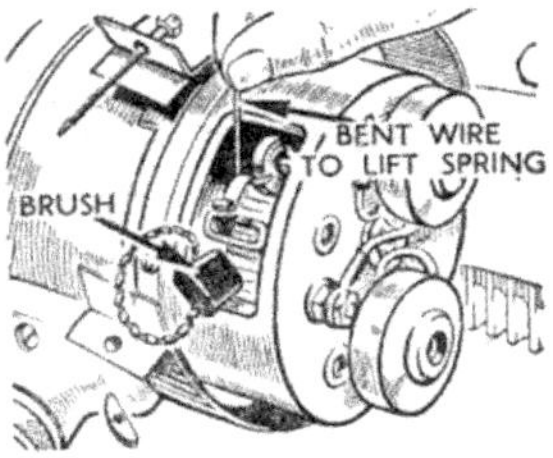

2. EXAMINE BRUSHES OF STARTER MOTOR, MAIN DYNAMO AND TURRET GENERATOR FOR WEAR AND CLEANLINESS. (ACCESS TO STARTER MOTOR THROUGH TRAP 2—SEE PAGE 60).
(*Job No. A.*16 *in Instruction Book*)

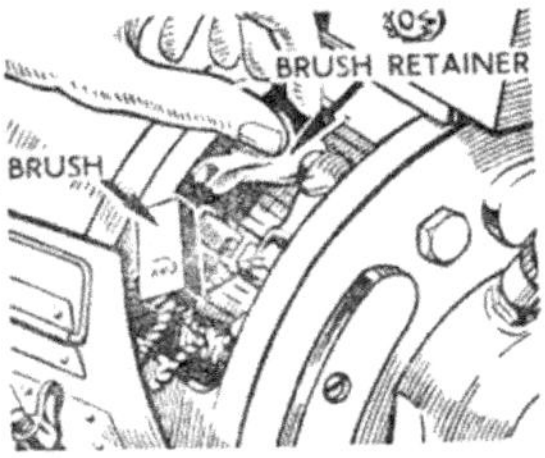

3. REMOVE FILTER DISCS FROM COMPRESSOR OUTLET FILTER, CLEAN THOROUGHLY IN PETROL AND REPLACE.
(*Job No. A.*15 *in Instruction Book*)

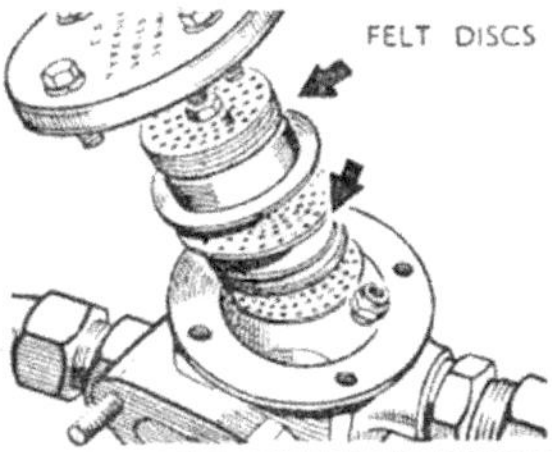

4. REMOVE, CLEAN AND RE-SET SPARKING PLUGS (GAP—.018 TO .020 IN.).
(*Job No. A.*9 *in Instruction Book*)

5. Drain sump of engine of auxiliary petrol electric generator and refill with engine oil (10 H.D.) to bottom thread of filler plug.
(*Job No. A.*2 *in Instruction Book*)

(*See illustration to item* 13, *page* 64).

LUBRICATION OPERATIONS ARE IN ORDINARY TYPE;

EVERY 1,000 MILES—continued

6. RENEW FLEXIBLE DRIVE SHAFT TO AMAL PUMP WHERE FITTED. TAKE GREAT CARE TO LOCATE THE CLIPS CORRECTLY SO THAT SHARP BENDS ARE AVOIDED. (ACCESS THROUGH TRAP 2—SEE PAGE 60).

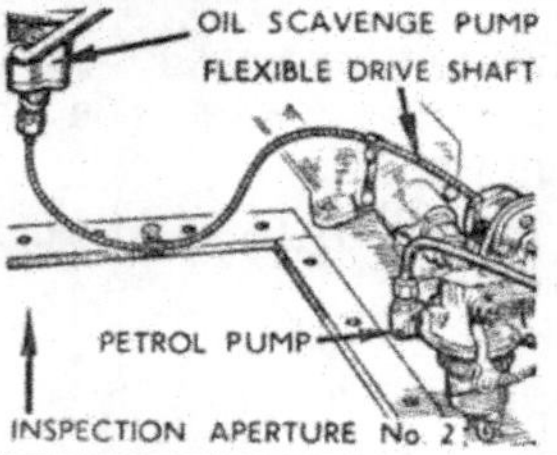

7. Lubricate idler wheels with gear oil (C.600) until oil exudes from the bearing. A nipple is provided on each idler for the pressure gun.

(*Job No. A.2 in Instruction Book*)

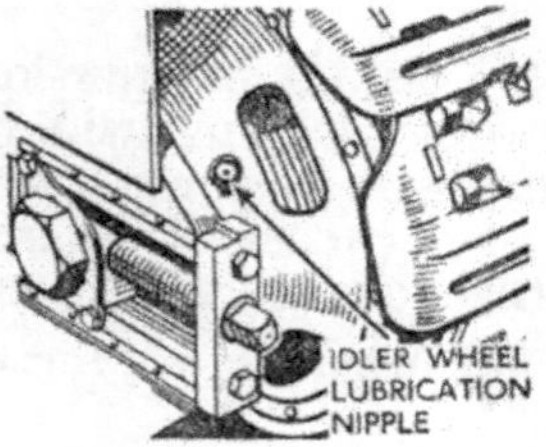

INSPECTIONS AND ADJUSTMENTS IN CAPITAL LETTERS

EVERY 2,000 MILES

1. Drain oil from gearbox and refill to level mark with gear oil (C.600). (Access to drain plug through Trap 1—see page 60). Allow time for the oil to find its level before checking by dipstick.

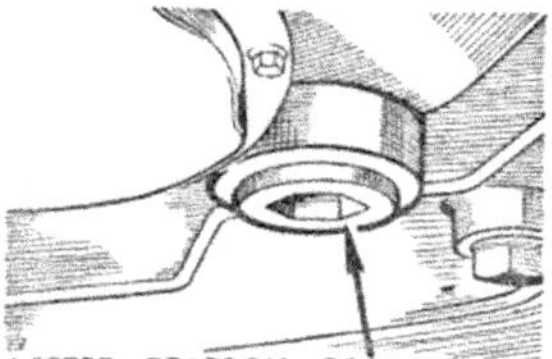

4-SPEED GEARBOX DRAIN PLUG

2. Oil distributor automatic mechanism (through holes in rotor arm) with engine oil (10 H.D.). Wipe arm dry after oiling.

(See illustration to item 3, page 73).

(Job No. A.2 in Instruction Book)

GENERAL HINTS AND TIPS

Don't drive fast on frozen, bumpy ground, or you may find the vehicle getting out of control.

* * *

Don't run with slack tracks if it can possibly be avoided. Slack tracks affect steering.

* * *

Watch the engine rev. counter when driving—and make sure the reading doesn't exceed 2,000 r.p.m. when going downhill.

* * *

If the CO_2 fire extinguisher bottles are used, obtain a replacement *immediately*.

* * *

The air servo motors are provided to make clutch and steering control easier. If the air pressure is lost, the vehicle can still be handled effectively without them although the controls will not be so light.

* * *

Don't attempt obstacle crossing or severe cross-country work with the petrol at a low level. Some of it is trapped when the vehicle is tilted, leaving the suction pipes high and dry.

* * *

Don't run with the cooling system short of water. Check frequently on *both* sides of the vehicle. A dry engine may mean cracked castings and blown gaskets.

* * *

Don't " ride " the clutch. The throw-out gear is air-assisted, and the air valve may open if the pedal is used as a foot-rest. Result—slipping and overheating.

* * *

Use a funnel for oil-filling. Spilt oil has often been mistaken for oil pipe leakage.

* * *

Open the water filler caps slowly after a run. The system operates under pressure, and a jet of steam or boiling water doesn't make a pleasant shower.

81

After checking and topping-up the oil level (especially after a long stand), run the engine for a few moments and then check the level again.

* * *

Handle the escape hatches carefully, and make sure they are securely fastened when open. If they drop on someone, they hurt.

* * *

Endeavour to keep the petrol economy light " out " when driving. This saves petrol.

* * *

Never turn the steering bar when the engine is running unless you desire to turn the vehicle.

* * *

Do not leave the vehicle parked, especially on a slope, with the hand-brake on only. Always engage a low gear.

* * *

Always close and lock the engine compartment hatches before moving off. This is necessary for correct engine cooling.

* * *

An accumulation of water or other fluids in the engine compartment can be cleared by opening the petrol dump valve. The control is in the fighting compartment.

* * *

The correct place for the tools is in the tool-box behind the driver's seat. More tools are lost by being left about the vehicle than are " scrounged " by other people.

* * *

Keep your tool equipment in good order. If a tool is damaged, report it and get a replacement. An inefficient tool is useless—and is not a good excuse for bad work.

* * *

When crossing obstacles meet them at right-angles whenever possible—this minimises side stress on the tracks.

* * *

Always remember that the Churchill is a heavy tank, and start from rest smoothly. A violent start imposes undue strains throughout the transmission.

Before starting, make sure that the two temperature indicators are recording. Both should indicate approximately 185° F. Remember, too, to keep an occasional eye on them while running. They will give warning of any fault developing in the cooling system.

* * *

Do not completely empty any petrol tank before changing over to another supply. The heavy suction caused when a tank is dry will overload the petrol pump drive. (This applies only to vehicles fitted with the *flexibly* driven Amal pump.)

* * *

Check the clutch pedal clearance daily. If the " free travel is not correct the clutch will slip. The " free travel " will vary very little if the clutch is properly used.

* * *

Always use "Lockheed Racing Green Fluid" or Hydraulic Brake Fluid No. 4 for topping-up the Lockheed systems. There is no permissible substitute.

* * *

When filling the water-systems or washing down the vehicle, try to prevent water accumulating in the engine compartment. This will be blown into the steering brakes by the fan, and the brakes will be ineffective until they are dried out.

RAIL TRANSPORT

Before transporting the Churchill Tank by rail the overall width must be reduced by removing the spare track plates, the tow rope shackle pins (unless they are welded into position) and the air inlet louvres. Details are given in the Instruction Book.

LUBRICATION CHART

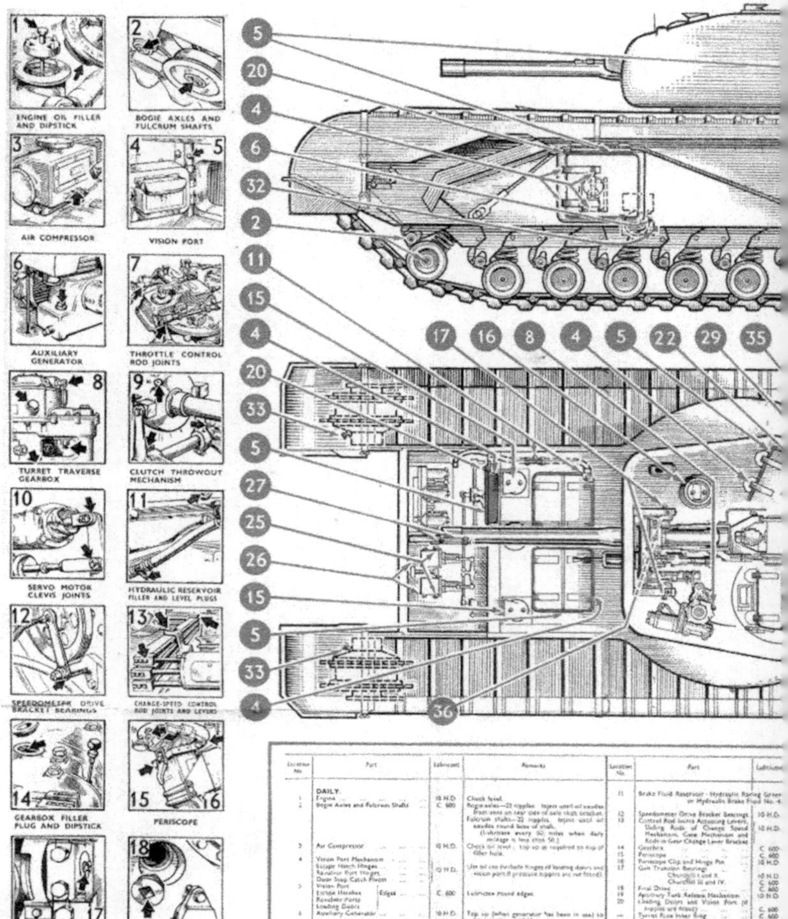

1. ENGINE OIL FILLER AND DIPSTICK

2. BOGIE AXLES AND FULCRUM SHAFTS

3. AIR COMPRESSOR

4–5. VISION PORT

6. AUXILIARY GENERATOR

7. THROTTLE CONTROL ROD JOINTS

8. TURRET TRAVERSE GEARBOX

9. CLUTCH THROWOUT MECHANISM

10. SERVO MOTOR CLEVIS JOINTS

11. HYDRAULIC RESERVOIR FILLER AND LEVEL PLUGS

12. SPEEDOMETER DRIVE BRACKET BEARINGS

13. CHANGE-SPEED CONTROL ROD JOINTS AND LEVERS

14. GEARBOX FILLER PLUG AND DIPSTICK

15–16. PERISCOPE

17. GUN TRUNNION BEARING

18. FINAL DRIVE FILLER PLUG

10 H.D. must be used for the engine if it can possibly be procured. In hot or temperate conditions 30 H.D.

CHURCHILL I, II, III & IV

AUXILIARY TANK RELEASE MECHANISM

LOADING DOOR NIPPLE

ENGINE DRAIN PLUG

AIR FILTER

GOVERNOR

TACHOMETER

STEERING SERVO CYLINDER

HAND BRAKE MECHANISM

AIR COMPRESSOR

MAIN GENERATOR

STARTER

AUXILIARY GENERATOR

IDLER WHEEL

GEARBOX DRAIN PLUG

DISTRIBUTOR AUTOMATIC MECHANISM

GUN DEPRESSION MECHANISM

used if 10 H.D. is not obtainable. In cold climates 30 H.D. is useless, and 10 H.D. MUST be used.

©2012 Periscope Film LLC
All Rights Reserved
ISBN#978-1-937684-73-0